THE IRANIAN MENACE in Jewish History and Prophecy

DR. JEFFREY L. SEIF

The Iranian Menace
In Jewish History and Prophecy

10300 North Central Expy Suite 170
Dallas, Texas 75231
214-696-8844
www.levitt.com

ISBN: 1930749600

Table of Contents

Table of Contents

*Eschatology: Religious doctrine dealing with death and the afterlife.

Table of Contents

*Eschatology: Religious doctrine dealing with death and the afterlife.

Foreword

Iran – Persia, a land of mystery, intrigue and many centuries of history. It is hard for us to believe today, but there was a time when Israel had no better friend in the world than Persia. That was when Cyrus was king, and he issued the decree that the Jewish people were to return to Jerusalem in order to rebuild the Temple. When other countries raised objection to the Jewish return, King Cyrus and his successor supported Israel. It's a different Iran (or Persia) today. Iran is a leader among the enemies of Israel now, publicly declaring that Israel should be wiped off the map, building up its nuclear capabilities and supporting terrorist organizations like Hezbollah and Hamas. It has joined the nations which have earned the description, "axis of evil."

Students of Bible prophecy have long been interested in Iran because of its mention in connection with the Gog and Magog War of Ezekiel 38-39 and the final war at the time of the Second Coming of Christ, Armageddon. This interest is not new. Jewish writers throughout the centuries have been describing Persia and its role in history and prophecy. Iran not only appears in the Bible, but in various commentaries and pseudepigrapha (works purporting to be biblical) as well. With this book, *The Iranian Menace in Jewish History and Prophecy*,

Dr. Jeffrey Seif has brought the voluminous information from these sources together into a veritable encyclopedia on the subject. His perspective, as a Jewish believer in Christ, has enabled him to research and compile those passages that bear on both Old and New Testament references to Iran, from Genesis to Revelation. This work will be particularly useful to scholars who want to cite some of the more obscure references to Iran as they prepare articles and books on the looming role of Iran in Biblical prophecy.

Dr. Seif here gathers together material from Jewish history, Roman history, apocalyptic and Messianic literature that mentions or develops the theme of Iran in the End Times, in the eschatological wars such as Gog and Magog and Armageddon, and in the Second Coming of the Lord Jesus Christ. All people interested in these subjects will appreciate the resource contribution made by this book.

Thomas S. McCall, Th.D.
Bullard, Texas
August 3, 2006

Introduction

Title

With militant Iran spewing out hot anti-American and anti-Israeli invective like lava, and with the imposing threat of that radical Islamic state's nuclear capabilities boiling just beneath the surface, I wondered whether there might be value in considering whether Iran has a role to play in the eruption of "end time" prophecy. Curious whether there was a relationship between Iran and the climactic showdown at "Armageddon," I combed through a variety of ancient biblical sources in search of an answer. This book, *The Iranian Menace in Jewish History and Prophecy,* contains my findings. When you read it, you will discover as I did that there's ample reason to be concerned with Iran.

A casual Internet search of the back-to-back words "Iran" and "Armageddon" turned up nearly 1,000,000 entries, evidence that people are beginning to consider a possible connection. That those people include a former presidential hopeful like Sen. John McCain, who explicitly said as much on "Meet the Press," and *The Washington Post* writer Charles Krauthammer, attests to the fact that concerns are not being raised only by "people at the fringes," as some would allege. By means of this volume, I am adding my name to the growing list of concerned individuals. In my case, however, I focused on a variety of *ancient* voices and not contemporary ones, important as they are.

Bible believers should keep an attentive eye on the militant Islamic, Iranian state, a point made apparent by media watchdog Joseph Farah in a recent worldnetdaily.com article, "Iran Leader's Messianic End-Times Mission." In that article he spoke of current Iranian President Mahmoud Ahmadinejad's personal interest in ushering in the Islamic version of the messianic era. With a videotaped meeting between President Ahmadinejad and the Ayatollah Javadi-Amoli in view, Farah recapped the president's candid discussion of "a strange, paranormal experience [that] he had while addressing the United Nations in New York." Ahmadinejad recounts how he found himself bathed in light… construed by the Iranian president to actually be "a light from heaven"—a divine endorsement for his spiritual calling. In a November 16, 2005 speech in Tehran, the president went on record expressing his interest in paving "the path for the glorious reappearance of Imam Mahdi," begging "may Allah hasten his reappearance." Who is Imam Mahdi? Islamic Shiites believe that "he will reign on earth for seven years, before bringing about a final judgment and the end of the world." *He is the Islamic Shiite Messiah.*

In his mind, President Ahmadinejad likens himself to Christianity's "John the Baptist"; for, like John, he envisions his role to be preparing the way for the Messiah—in his case Islam's messianic lord![1] In his UN speech Ahmadinejad made

[1] "There's [even] a new messiah hotline [set up]. There are news agencies especially devoted to the latest developments," reports Farah. Leaning on Ali Lari, of the Bright Future Institute in the Iranian religious center of Qom, he goes on to note that "People are anxious to know when and how will He rise; [and] what they must do to receive this worldwide

his perceived role clear when he called for the "mighty Lord" to hasten "the promised one" and to "fill this world with justice and peace" at his coming.

Problematic for Ahmadinejad—and for many other Muslims—is the perception that the American "West" is standing in the way of that impending, Islamic messianic era.[2] Wanting to facilitate the arrival of the purified Islamic world order, and perceiving that Israel and her allies are contaminated obstacles that need to be removed, might Islamic elements from the "East" vent their misguided religious zeal on Israel and the "West"? Could these strong religious impulses eventually propel frenzied radicals into a major war, possibly even "Armageddon"? Leaning on Iranian journalist Hossein Bastan, Charles Krauthammer in *The Washington Post* (December 16, 2005) reported Ahmadinejad's belief that the impending Islamic messianic era will dawn within two years. This belief gives rise to the likelihood that Ahmadinejad's plan to develop nuclear energy is not for domestic use alone.

Style and Method

As a concerned *American*, as a *Jewish* believer in Jesus, and as a professionally trained *Christian* theologian, I have often found myself pressed between a variety of distinct-yet-related

---

salvation." That this is reasonably widespread is evidenced by Iranian theologians' claims that 20% of Iranians are interested in prophecy: "Shiite writings [are said to] describe events surrounding the return of the Mahdi in apocalyptic terms" and "Ahmadinejad's repeated invocation of Imam Mahdi['s appearance], known as 'the Savior of Times'… [to facilitate the] Judgment Day [and] to herald a truly just government." (Culled from worldnetdaily.com, article ID 48225.)

[2] How so? "A top priority of Ahmadinejad is 'to challenge America, which is trying to impose itself as the final salvation of the human being, and insert its unjust state [in the region],' says Hamidreza Taraghi, head of the conservative Islamic Coalition Society. Taraghi says the U.S. is 'trying to place itself as the new Mahdi.'"

worlds. Weighing them together as I do stimulates creative work-product: in this case, a book like the one you're reading in which various ancient *Christian* and *Jewish* concerns intersect with modern, real- world problems and possibilities. To complement fast-coming Middle East news, I will attempt to show in this narrative that ancient biblical and post-biblical writers alike envisioned trouble at day's end from an evil empire east of the Euphrates, with Israel drawn into its center. In formally presenting my historical research for your consideration, my aim will be to calmly offer well-reasoned, clearly-stated and simply-put answers to the previously-posited question of Iran's place in the quagmire—a job that, I grant, may seem a bit "easier said than done."

American poet Walt Whitman once noted: "[T]he glory of expression… is simplicity." With that as my guide, I aim to present a "user-friendly" text, accessible to both beginners and advanced Bible students alike.[3] With that in mind, I will keep technical academic jargon to a minimum; "esoteric" terms will be followed immediately by explanations in the text or in a footnote at the bottom of the page.[4] Reference materials, expansions and other conventions of formal academic inquiry will be noted in the footnotes, as well. While the academic apparatus will be discernable and available to those interested in my expansions and sources,[5] I will endeavor to keep the main text reasonably uncluttered.

---

[3] I have been a Bible college professor at Christ for the Nations Institute, Dallas, since the summer of 1989. My new post as the principal spokesperson in Zola Levitt's wake forces me to creatively employ ways to speak more clearly, to the broader culture and not just to college students.

[4] "Esoteric," for example, means "intended for the initiated," and references technical language used by specialists and barely intelligible to non-specialists.

[5] For this reason I opted to employ footnotes at the page's bottom rather than endnotes, which are placed at the rear of the book. Interested readers

Introduction

To use a biblical term, I want to be a "*watchman* on the wall,"[6] informing my readers on grave matters that may not be on their daily radar. Pastors primarily instruct on a host of life-related issues, like marriage and family matters, child rearing, finances, and personal holiness. Distinct from what local pastors do, I want to use my platform as a television spokesperson with a international audience of millions to bring biblical insights to matters that affect our culture, Israel, and the world at large. In the process, I want to lead people both to and through some new and interesting material; to offer reasoned and sensible accountings of things there were

---

need only glance to the bottom of the page for more information, instead of having to find the sources in the book's rear.

6 In Scripture, readers encounter sentinels (or "watchmen") posted to protect citizens from plundering hordes of invaders. Some prophets were even construed and commissioned as "watchmen." Situated precariously on the only over-land trade routes connecting Africa, Arabia and Europe, those in the ancient Israelite nation-state knew all too well the importance of posting vigilant "watchmen." The Greek noun "phulake," denoting a "night watchman," is used in Lk. 2:8; Mt. 14:25; 24:43; Mk. 6:48, and was construed as a vocation akin to being "koustodia," (i.e., to have "custody"), as with Mt. 27:65-66. "Keeping watch," or "tereo," is noted in conjunction with the guards/watchers, in Mt. 27:36, 54, much as "gregoreo" is used to speak of being spiritually "watchful," "awake" and "alert," as in Mt. 24:43; 26:38 and Acts 20:31. A statement made famous for New Testament readers by Paul— that "the just shall live by faith" (Rom. 1:17)—is itself culled from a re-employed Habakkuk text, where the prophet says: "I will stand my watch and set myself on the rampart" after which he gives voice to faith (2:1). Habakkuk's "watch" (Heb. "mismeret") was an "observation station," and his "rampart" (Heb. "masor") was a "watchtower" or "fortress." As noted, I believe that ministries such as Zola Levitt's are instrumental in calling individuals' attention to major events of biblical proportions. While pastors are uniquely positioned to address biblical issues related to their constituents' personal lives, television ministries (as with Zola's and now mine by association) are uniquely positioned to draw attention to prophetic concerns that have broad-sweeping consequences.

(historic) and of things that will be (prophetic). This is my objective. Some say it's too ambitious, believing that the issues are too complex and the material too far removed from the grasp of the average person. I wish to prove them wrong, and I want you to help me.

Talking plainly about prophecy and fulfillment was my predecessor Zola Levitt's[7] trademark, much as plain speech was valued by the Apostle Paul who noted: "[I]f the trumpet makes an uncertain sound, who will prepare for [the] battle?" (1 Cor. 14:8) If I understand the Apostle correctly, Paul believed that it was useless to call attention to an impending crisis if he, the "watchman" on a wall, drew attention in a way that others could not grasp. Tragically, this "hard to grasp" manner seems characteristic in a lot of today's theological language.

Though Paul was the premiere and only professionally-trained theologian in the early Messianic-Jewish movement, he seemed particularly casual in his approach to communicating and ministering: [8] he was "reader friendly,"[9] if you will. Such is my desire.

---

[7] Though some may come upon this volume by other means, it was principally written for, and presented under the auspices of, Zola Levitt Ministries (a television concern) where I serve as the principal theologian and Bible teacher since Zola's passing.

[8] Writing in his Reenvisioning Theological Education (Grand Rapids: Eerdmans Pub. 1999), Dr. Robert Banks noted that the "language of collegiality [and] of partnership" is particularly noteworthy in the various Pauline correspondences and practices, over and against the formal, European-based, university-type techno-nonsense that seems to prevail in theological communication and academia today. By contrast, as stated, Paul was particularly "down to earth," and had a way of relating to many individuals directly.

[9] Upwards of 40 people are known to have traveled and worked alongside Paul. Included in the cosmopolitan group of workers were Jews (Acts

Introduction

Content

My opening chapter is entitled "The *Case for* the Iranian-Armageddon Connection in Jewish History and Prophecy." It contains my fundamental assumptions, methods, and conclusions. With those both noted and developed, I follow with "The *Place of* the Iranian-Armageddon Connection in Ancient Jewish and Roman Histories," where I offer historical samplings of how Jews and Romans in a bygone era addressed what both construed as impending Iranian crises. In that chapter I attempt to strengthen the evidence alluded to in the previous chapter. Having looked at the "case" and the "place," I follow with a third section entitled "The *Space for* the Iranian-Armageddon Connection in Ancient Apocalyptic Literature." Relying on a host of ancient Jewish sources, I briefly consider prophetic impulses in the ancient Jewish world and I sketch out how many prophecy-oriented Jewish Bible teachers understood the "last days'" world in relation to their own worlds—to Israel and to western (Roman) culture, particularly. I note how various Jewish seers and biblical commentators pictured the eventual emergence and displacement of a wicked world ruler who would mobilize his forces in and around modern Iran, from which this diabolical leader would then assault the world in a fantastic end-time drama. Having addressed the historical and prophetic concerns

---

4:36; 15:22; 18:3,8) and non-Jews alike (Acts 16:10; 19:29; 20:4), as well as folk of mixed ethnic backgrounds (Acts 16:1). Though men predominated, women were included as helpers as well (Rom. 16:6-15; Philem. 1:2), as were younger singles, married folk and older widows (Acts 18:1-3). The young and the old were noted (1 Tim. 4:12; 2 Tim. 2:22), as were masters and servants, the rich and the poor (Col. 4:1,9; Philem. 1:8-21). For the aforementioned reasons, Banks says that Paul "crossed the religious, ethnic, gender and status lines in a way that was unparalleled at that time." Taking my lead from both my predecessor Zola Levitt and the ancient "rabbi-turned-reverend" named Paul, I too am minded to be as reader-friendly as possible—and may God help me in my endeavor.

in the "case," "place" and "space" chapters, I go on to offer reflections on "The *Face of* Jesus in the Iranian-Armageddon Conflict and in Ancient Jewish Eschatology," principally by assessing Jesus' explicit statements in the book of Revelation.

This final "face" chapter, offers an abbreviated assessment of the four hundred and three verses in Revelation, with pride of place given to the sixty-three "red letter" verses attributed directly to Jesus. Noteworthy is the fact that Jesus doesn't pull out prophecy charts for "arm chair" theologians with prophecy interests. Rather, He imposes practical instructions upon His hearers' minds—instructions worth a fresh hearing today. What is particularly striking in Revelation is that the description of a last days war—replete with a heinously wicked end-time ruler venting his fury on persecuted saints, and of the Messiah's victorious coming at the end to vanquish the foe and establish the heavenly kingdom—is *not* unique to the book of Revelation: these notions are found and developed in other literature and later in this book. What is unique to Jesus—and thus to the actual "Revelation" of Jesus in the book by that name—are the practical, non-ethereal instructions given to believers, all of which instruct not to be too distracted but to keep with the mission, to keep holy in an unholy world, and to keep optimistic. The practical, ministry-related implications of prophecy will be explored in conjunction with this, in my closing chapter.

Sources Used

Having briefly considered my title and my primary purpose in writing, and after explaining the style and framework of this book, a word about the ancient Jewish sources is in order, particularly because many of my readers might not be familiar with some of them. I'll begin with a source familiar to most: the Sacred Scripture.

As you will see here and throughout this book, the Scriptures factor most significantly in my understanding and in my writing.[10] I hold them in the highest regard as God's very Word. Thus I see great value in the inspired light they shed on everything including the historical and spiritual concerns we will confront in this book. In order to expose my readers to "Jewish" perspectives on those very Scriptures, I use the Jewish Publication Society of America's English rendition of the Hebrew Old Testament text (instead of, say, the King James Version[11]), much as I will confine myself to using standard non-Christian, Jewish sources in that Hebrew Bible's analysis. I will look at some of the Old Testament's premiere authors—like Isaiah, Ezekiel and Zechariah—whose words contain particularly insightful eschatological, or end-times, importance. After noting the standard Jewish translations of their respective Old Testament texts, I will then consider how some ancient Jewish theologians construed those prophets' words. By limiting my scope to traditional Jewish text and commentators this way, I hope to introduce readers to decidedly Jewish perspectives, ones which will dovetail nicely with Christian ones—as I trust you shall see as we go.

In summary, I want you to hear from both the Jewish translation and the Jewish interpretation of the Hebrew Scriptures. I think that you'll find this particularly insightful, and that you will be pleasantly surprised to note how the *New*

---

[10] Unless otherwise noted, I will be using the New King James Version.

[11] As you will note in the text, my doing so is not born out of any belief that this version is better than the Christian versions, but rather my belief that the Jewish rendition might help readers be better acquainted with Jewish views, which is my primary intention. For those who are curious, I usually use the New King James Version of the Sacred Scriptures, personally.

Testament authors handled prophecy in a manner that was very consistent with the biblical Jewish writers and their various post-biblical Jewish interpreters.

Speaking of Jewish sources, let me interject that I believe the New Testament to be an extremely Jewish book, given that it is a story about a Jew named Jesus, who preached to Jewish people in the Jewish language, and who ministered to Jews in the Jewish homeland—Israel. The New Testament specifies that He taught in Jewish synagogues and that He spoke about a very Jewish subject—the "Messiah." Noted, as well, is the fact that the early Jesus movement's most ardent advocate, Paul, was himself a Torah-observant "rabbi" who came to faith in Jesus as Israel's promised Messiah. For these and other reasons, I am personally very comfortable describing the New Testament as a Jewish book and source, despite the fact that a number of my Jewish friends may object.[12] Anticipated objections notwithstanding, I frankly perceive the New Testament to be an extremely valuable source of Jewish understanding, as it sheds light on first-century Jewish language, history and more. As noted before, I will be using the New King James Version.

So much for biblical sources.

Next, Professor G. A. Williamson's translation of Josephus' *The Jewish War*[13] is of particular interest to me. This important, first- century Jewish author was a contemporary of some of the New Testament writers, and was himself a competent

---

[12] For that matter, let me note that while attending to New Testament texts, I will speak as a Jewish theologian—albeit a Messianic Jewish one.

[13] Known to most originally as Bellum Judaicum, Josephus' work has been ably reproduced in English thanks to the work of Dr. Williamson, with notes and appendixes upgraded by Dr. E. Mary Smallwood. (See The Jewish War [New York: Dorset Press, 1981]).

Jewish historian of significant repute.[14] Josephus had much to say about Iran's incursions into Judea and its meddling with Judean and Roman political affairs, incidents that had direct bearing on the New Testament's first-century Jewish and Roman political worlds—of which more will be said later.

In Josephus' day, the nation occupying the Iranian landmass was known as "Parthia"—not Iran. In her introduction to her translation of Josephus' *Jewish War*, Dr. E. Mary Smallwood noted that Josephus even "wrote it first in Aramaic for circulation among the Jews of the eastern Diaspora—those living beyond the Euphrates and under Parthian rule—but [that Josephus] later translated the classic book into Greek, in order to make it accessible to the peoples of the Roman empire."[15] It is worth noting that Josephus was very much interested in people who lived in what is now modern-day Iran. He says as much in his own opening section: "Parthians, Babylonians, Southern Arabians… thanks to my labors were accurately informed of the causes of the [Jewish] war."[16] Similarly, I believe that we do well to be informed by Josephus on bygone Iranian/Parthian struggles with Israel and with Rome, thus the purpose for this subsection.

In addition to employing biblical references and Josephus' historical treatment of Iran/Parthia, we will consider a host of other first-century sources.

---

[14] And disrepute too, because he abandoned the revolt and went over to the Romans.
[15] Ibid., p. 14.
[16] Ibid., p. 72.

Ancient pseudepigraphical[17] writers who offered additional commentary on Iran (known to them as "Parthia" and "Persia") and to the Jewish understanding of prophecy will also be considered. By so doing, we open a broad window through which we can glimpse how biblical interpreters in the ancient world felt and thought. I expect that readers will find this particularly interesting for a variety of reasons which will surface later.

Dr. George W. Macrae, a professor at Harvard University, expressed the belief that pseudepigraphical literature augments New Testament studies because the ancient literature helps students understand ancient Judaic eschatological idioms—Jewish "last days" language. He says: We need to know "as much [as we can] about the [New Testament] Biblical world in all of its facets." Along with Professor Macrae, I believe that apocryphal and pseudepigraphical literature—from the Gnostic Nag Hammadi codices[18] to the Dead Sea Scrolls, and various ancient extracts preserved solely in Christian Syriac, Greek, Ethiopic and Latin translations—satisfy this need quite nicely; and with him, I am convinced that anyone interested in New Testament studies is well served by becoming acquainted with the non-canonical works, both for the sake of the works themselves, and for the light they shed on the ancient New Testament world and vocabulary.[19] Most

---

17 Using a million-dollar word like "pseudepigrapha" just after promising that I wouldn't employ excessively technical vocabulary may well test the patience of my readers. Let me say that the word simply means "written under another name", a pseudonym. I plan to steer away from, or at least explain, technical jargon, but I use this one now as an entrance to the information that follows.

18 A collection of ancient texts found in Nag Hammadi, Egypt.

19 In fact, no modern conservative evangelical theologian ignores it (The Use of the Bible in Theology: Evangelical Options, ed. Robert K. Johnston [Atlanta: John Knox Press, 1985])

evangelical exegetes,[20] in fact, work with these sources and see doing so as a necessary prerequisite to proper biblical interpretation.[21]

What will you discover in the following pages? Our cursory examination of pseudepigraphical literature will turn up evidence that the New Testament's "Battle of Armageddon" appears beyond the pages of the New Testament. You will also see that expressions like "Son of Man," "Tribulation Period," "Heaven," "End times," "Hell," "Judgment Day," "New Heaven" and "New Earth" were in common use amongst the Jews in and around Jesus' day. Because most Christians first confront these expressions in the New Testament, many assume that they are the exclusive property of the New Testament. This misperception will be clarified; as we shall see, these Judaic expressions were part of the Jewish vocabulary outside the community of Jesus' immediate followers. They sprang from a common source that ancient Jews and the original Jesus followers—themselves Jews—held in common: the Old Testament.

Ancient Jews had a Bible. Like all cultures, Jews developed a vocabulary through which they articulated their understanding of their world and, in their case, gave a theological accounting of events within that world—past, present and future. Jesus came and spoke to Jewish people using that preexisting vocabulary and imagery, a language that came replete with maxims and mental images reflecting an underlying biblical theology and an eschatology already in vogue amongst Jews. In His parables, Jesus used existing vocabulary to instruct His

---

20 Exegetes give critical explanations of Scripture.

21 Use of the Bible in Theology: Evangelical Options, above.

Judean followers.[22] Likewise, He employed existing Jewish eschatological language—Jewish expressions of "last days" events predicted in the Bible—to speak of the coming Kingdom and beyond. We should not be surprised by all of this, though I know you will be, as I was at first; for, why wouldn't the New Testament contain many prevailing Judaic expressions, given the Jewish nature of the literature, itself. To summarize, *the non-canonical pseudepigraphical genre enables us to better understand that idiom;* this, in turn, aids students of the New Testament by making the language of Jesus and Paul more intelligible to modern Christian and Jewish readers alike. Don't get sidetracked if this seems too technical. It will become clearer to you when we actually get into it.

Moving along, and focusing explicitly on Iranian-related ancient literature, we will look at Princeton scholar Dr. James H. Charlesworth's *Old Testament Pseudepigrapha: Apocalyptic Literature and Testaments.*[23] A number of its references to Iran will be noted—but under the ancient name of "Parthia," as with Josephus above. Of these, we will focus particularly on the "last days," eschatologically[24] dominated *Sibylline Oracles*, which shed light upon how ancient Romans and Jews viewed the "east," and how they construed that the final "last days" war would be stimulated by agitation and movement from the east—from modern-day Iran, particularly. Dr. J. J. Collins,

---

22 On this score, I'm pleased to recommend Dr. Brad Young's work in the field. In particular, I found The Jewish Background to the Lord's Prayer (Dayton: Center for Judeo-Christian Studies, 1984) to be quite helpful, as well as Jesus and His Jewish Parables (New York: Paulist Press, 1989).

23 Edited by Charlesworth, the two-volume set I use, entitled Old Testament Pseudepigrapha, was published by Doubleday, out of Garden City, NY, in 1983.

24 "Eschatology," in Christian language/nomenclature, denotes "last things" and refers to end-time Bible prophecy.

professor of Religious Studies at De Paul University,[25] Chicago, offers his translations and comments, which I will use and consider in this section.

By way of further introduction, note that many of these Sibylline speakers were themselves residents of what would be present-day Iran. They were "Asiatic… and are widely assumed to have come to Greece from the East,"[26] with first place given to the oracles[27] from Iran/Parthia, whose prophesies relevant to humankind's "final age" (*ultima aetas*) say that the end-time war will one day be played out against the backdrop

---

25 I will refer to authors by the titles and positions they held at the time of their publication noted. It may well be that some have moved to other positions within their colleges and/or to other schools; some may well have retired altogether.

26 "Sibylline Oraces" in Old Testament Pseudepigrapha, Vol. I, p. 317.

27 These "oracles" have surfaced at interesting times and in interesting places in the "West," as evidenced by the following story. In 1475, Pope Sixtus IV commissioned Pontelli to design the Vatican's "palace chapel." Thirty-three years later, Pope Julius II called upon a budding artist named Michelangelo to leave his mark on the chapel's ceiling. Though already engaged in constructing Pope Julius II's tomb, Michelangelo accepted the additional commission, commenced with the project, worked on it with dogged determination, and finished it on 02 November 1512. Decorated with various episodes from Scripture, Michelangelo's famous ceiling tells of mankind's rise and demise, of the race's descent into depravity and of its ascent through the Messiah's triumph on humankind's behalf. Rooted in Italian Renaissance culture, Michelangelo employed a variety of non-biblical sources, as well, in telling the story. Colossal "Ignudi" ("nudes") are found throughout, as are depictions of sibyls—all intermixed with famous biblical prophets. Paired opposite Jonah, for example, is the Sibyl of Lybia; the prophet Daniel is observed opposite the Cumaean Sibyl; Isaiah is paired with the Delphic Sibyl, and so forth. All in all, twelve prophets and non-biblical luminaries alternate on the chapel's lateral walls, all of whom are depicted as peering intensely into the future. Their doing so arguably harks to man's restless quest to know the future and to look for redemption in it—an interest shared by biblical prophet and sibylline commentator alike.

of Iran/Parthia's bold entrance into the world's "final conflict," being led by a warring, demonic figure. This story is very much akin to the Armageddon scenario noted in the book of Revelation.

Beyond the Scriptures, Josephus and the Sibyls, we will look at *1 Enoch* (also referred to by the title *Ethiopic Apocalypse of Enoch*), as translated by Dr. E. Isaac, visiting professor at Bard College. Duke University Professor O. S. Wintermute's translation of the *Apocalypse of Elijah* is considered, also a scholar from the Netherlands, Dr. A. F. J. Klijn's translation of *2 Baruch*.

The books listed above offer *insights to help us understand the fantastic and highly-charged language of prophecy in general, and the ancients' understanding of Iran's place in world-end prophecy in particular.*[28] This book can be used with other resources, such as those offered by our and other ministries, that are designed to help each of us reconcile the world in which we live with the Word we love to read. In our ministry's monthly *Levitt Letter*—which I suggest you acquire if you haven't done so already—our staff pulls together the best modern commentary we can find on contemporary Middle East news in order to keep our ministry friends up on breaking news. Unlike the *Levitt Letter*, this book makes Spartan use of modern commentary as here I prefer to draw upon ancient sources which, in their own way, mesh with today's news. We who are looking for a spiritual perspective on current events can be reassured by these ancient texts that history is not spiraling out of control, but is, in fact,

28 Abbreviated though my introduction may well be, I hope that the above will suffice as an introductory treatment of my primary sources. Throughout the work, other historical works will be consulted; and serious readers are exhorted to note the sources in the subtext, should they want further information.

being guided by a powerful God and being led toward an eventual happy resolution, at His Son's imminent coming.

Though it all may sound very complex—and in certain respects it is—I will strive to minimize technical jargon and make the above accessible to everyone.

Speaking of both "complex" and "everyone," let me point out that this book does not delve into complicated prophecy-fulfillment scenarios and debates, and that it is designed to appeal to a variety of individuals with differing prophecy perspectives. Because my primary purpose is to introduce readers to ancient Jewish approaches to prophecy and to how Iran factored into it, modern theories, end time formulas, date settings, and debates among Christians are not taken up here, though you may want to pursue their study after reading this book.

Special Thanks

Before moving ahead, let me give special thanks to a number of individuals who have assisted me in various ways. I am indebted to Ken Berg, Sandra Levitt and Mark Levitt with whom I work closely in my new role as the principal presenter for Zola Levitt Ministries. Without their support, I would not be bringing this work to you under the auspices of Zola Levitt Ministries. Special thanks, also, to ZLM's editor Margot Dokken and Aaron Levitt who helped with the manuscript.

I am indeed thankful that my wife Patty and sons Jacob and Zachary had given me leave to pursue my vision of becoming a Messianic Jewish theologian. I thought there was value in becoming one—though I frankly never envisioned it would eventually bring me to assume the lead role in a internationally-known television ministry. Were it not for God's grace and my family's support, it would have never happened at all. Without their giving me permission to pursue my sometimes hard-to-comprehend dreams, I would not now be finishing this book's introduction from the Prima Royale hotel in Jerusalem, itself a reasonably short distance from the "Wailing Wall." Yesterday I finished shooting an eight-part television series on Isaiah, which we filmed in and around Jerusalem. Though "I am off" today, the film crew is still quite busy; thus I am able to retire to my room alone and focus on bringing this book to a close. That Christ for the Nations Institute in Dallas gave me leave from teaching as an adjunct in the full summer term is appreciated, as is Resurrection Life Church's graciously granting me leave from pastoral duties there. Beyond all this, let me say that I have been assisted by many others as well. I beg their pardon for any negligent omissions. And while speaking of negligence, I take full responsibility for any and all inadvertent errors located herein. I tried to be responsible; but I make no claim to perfection and have accepted that, try though we may, error is and will remain part of the human condition. Pardon is humbly requested in advance.

Having unpacked some of the book's particulars, and having thanked those who have assisted me in bringing those particulars to you, I now invite you to examine the first chapter and discover that there is more to Iran than you may have realized.

Jeffrey L. Seif
June 2006 Jerusalem

I

The *Case for* the Iranian-Armageddon Connection in Jewish History and Prophecy

Introducing Iran in History

Let's state the fundamental question—and its facets: (1) Did Iran play a role in biblical history in the Old Testament and New Testament eras? (2) Will Iran play a role in the fulfillment of modern biblical prophecy, in the possibly not-too-distant future? (3) Is there a connection between Iran and Armageddon? The answer is "yes" on all three counts, as you shall see. At the outset, I must inform you that Iran played a role in biblical history under another name.[1]

In New Testament times, Iran was known as "Parthia" (Acts 2:9), much as it was known as "Persia" in the era of the Old

[1] Though known today as "Jomhuri-ye Eslami-ye Iran" (the "Islamic Republic of Iran") and referred to as the political entity presently inextricably entrenched on the 634,734 square mile parcel east of the Euphrates and Tigris rivers in southwestern Asia, the land was known to the ancients much earlier as "Parthia" in New Testament and as "Persia" during part of Old Testament times, and not by the present appellation "Iran."

Testament prophet Daniel (Dan. 10:13). Of interest to us is "Parthia," and particularly what I will refer to as "Iran/Parthia" to underscore in the mind's eyes of my readers that the ancient geographical location is currently known as the Iranian nation-state.

Recorded history begins with a record of Elamites settling on the Iranian/Parthian tract approximately 3,000BC, followed eventually by Indo-Europeans, who successfully forged kingdoms in the region around 2,000BC. The Medes followed and flourished, holding sway over the Iranian land mass from 728-550BC, till they were overthrown by the Persians under Cyrus II. In 356BC, Phillip of Macedon sired a son whom he named Alexander. After ascending to his father's throne, Alexander crossed the Hellespont to exact the vengeance of Greece upon the Persians. Persian rule ended with Alexander the Great's bold and glorious conquests, executed during his short but successful lifetime. The Greek state that followed Alexander in the region, however, was eventually undone by the Parthians, who ruled at the eastern fringe of the empire from 247BC till 224AD—for nearly 500 years, right into New Testament times. Though they proved themselves quite capable of holding the western Romans at bay—as we'll see later—over time, incessant wars with Rome weakened the Parthians, with the result that the region passed to the Sasanians. Wars with Christian Byzantines weakened their empire further, affording Arab Muslims the opportunity to seize control of the land by 640AD, with the result that, for the following 850 years, the Iranian land mass was controlled by *non*-Iranian, Islamic princes—as at the present time.

Discontent over the last prince, Mozaffar od-Din Shah, culminated in a coup that brought Reza Khan to power in 1921, and resulted in Mozaffar finally being unseated in 1925. Reza Khan collaborated with the Nazis in WWII and, after

Germany's inglorious end, he was forced to abdicate power to his son, Mohammad Reza "Shah" Pahlavi. Wanting to both placate and align himself with Western powers, the "Shah" lost the popular, street-level support needed to govern. As a result, he was eventually unseated by a popular uprising in 1979, one led by Ruhollah Khomeini, an "ayatollah" who returned from exile in Paris and set up the country's present-day "Islamic Republic."[2] In an interview with Dubai-based Al-Arabiya TV, the late Grand Ayatollah's discontented grandson, Ayatollah Hussein Khomeini, referred to present-day Iran as a nation run by "a dictatorship of clerics who control every aspect of life."[3] This authoritarian Islamic republic is currently led by President Mahmoud Ahmadinejad, a virulently anti-Western and anti-Israeli[4] man, bent on bringing the medieval-type, religiously inclined, totalitarian[5] Iranian kingdom into the "nuclear

---

[2] See "Iran" in *The New Encyclopaedia Britannica*, pp. 374-376.

[3] Culled from "Tehran," in *The Week* (June 23, 2006), p. 11.

[4] In a recent interview with the German periodical *Der Spiegel*, Ahmadinejad expressed that he is unconvinced that a holocaust of Jews ever happened in Europe and wondered "Why do European countries commit themselves to defending the [Israeli occupation] regime" in the wake of what he tacitly posits to be an historical myth. President Ahmadinejad then stated that "the German people have been taken captive by the Zionists" for their uncritical acceptance. (The interview was conducted by Stefan Auts, Gerhard Sporl and Dieter Bednarz in Tehran and was posted on Tuesday, May 30th 2006.)

[5] Made up of many peoples today, nearly half Iran's citizens are native Iranians or Persians, with the remainder of the population divided amongst folk of Kurdish descent, semi-nomadic Lurs, Bakhtyari tribes in the Zagros mountains, and Armenians with European affinities. Many are young people, and most are indeed quite decent people. Though diverse, diversity is not allowed in Iran—as in other totalitarian, Islamic countries. The constitution of the present Islamic Republic of Iran vests political power in the *valiye-faqih*, the leading theologian and philosophical and political guardian. The country's leading individual or council commands the army, approves presidential candidates, appoints judges and appoints

age"—what seems to me to make for a very scary combination.

As we shall see immediately below, Iran's "coming into her own" in the modern world—under the relatively new banner of the present-day "Islamic Republic of Iran"—seems to have happened about the same time that Arab nationals decided to extricate themselves from European-based colonial controls. Anxious to throw off Western imperialist influences, Arab nationals asserted their prerogatives in and around the region and successfully forged their own autonomous Arabic states by the dint of their dogged determination, culminating in the emergence of the area's "Arab League" of states.[6] Beginning at the northern-most part of Africa and moving eastward across northern Africa and well into Arabia, we will briefly note how this was the case.

Morocco, located at the western end of North Africa, became an independent state in 1956, after being extricated from the European French and Spanish protectorate held over it since 1912. Situated immediately to Morocco's east is Algeria. After becoming a French holding in 1842, Algeria likewise became an independent Arab republic in 1962. Tunisia did much the same in 1975, having been a French holding since 1883. Moving eastward still, one comes upon Libya, which had

---

clerical members to the "Council of Guardians," a body responsible for seeing that all government policies conform to Islam. The Islamic Republican Party controls the courts, as religious jurists sit on the Supreme Court and the High Council of the Judiciary. The press is controlled by the Islamic Republic News Agency. For all these reasons, it is referred to as a "totalitarian" regime.

[6] Given the relatively new creation and re-alignment of Arab powers, one wonders why those powers would begrudge Jews from doing likewise—as with the establishment of the nation of Israel during the same historical season.

been brought into the Italian fold in 1912. Libya, however, was later superintended by a joint Anglo-French rule in 1945, following WWII, till securing its independence in 1951. Neighboring Egypt was under the British protectorate since 1914; Egypt, however, became an independent kingdom in 1922, and then finally a republic in 1953. Just to Egypt's south, Sudan became an independent republic in 1956, having been governed by joint Anglo-Egyptian rule since 1889. Just to Egypt's north and east is the country of Lebanon, which was under the French mandate of 1920, till it became an independent republic in 1944, much as its neighbor Syria was under the 1920 French mandate till it secured autonomy in 1943. In like manner, modern Jordan was under the French mandate of 1920, till becoming independent in 1946. Iraq became an independent kingdom in 1921 and a republic in 1958. Saudi Arabia secured its independence in 1927, as did Yemen in 1962.[7]

The modern Arab aversion to anything that smacks of European control may well stem from their experiences while emerging as independent Arab States, laboring to extricate themselves from European, colonial controls. Seeing the United Nations' sanctioning of Israel in 1947 as another example of European meddling in what they perceive as "their world"—and one vouchsafed to them by Allah, no less—Israel's existence is typically and naturally construed by Arabs as the left-over fruits of an old and vanquished imperialist system. It is thus seen as a wrong needed to be made right in world history, and as an insult needing the remedy of religion. Arabs pay no mind to biblical prophecy calling for Israel's emergence at day's end, but see the presence of Israel's

---

[7] See "The Arab League Since 1945" in Martin Gilbert's *Atlas of Jewish History*, p. 116.

nation-state as a reprehensible insult, a wrong needing to be righted by Allah himself.

Never mind the fact that the Israelites entered Canaan after the "Exodus" in the fifteenth century BC, and held it till the middle of the second century AD. Never mind that when Arab Muslims overran Jerusalem in 638AD Christians had ruled the city for three hundred years. It is futile to point out the details or attempt to reason, for many prefer just to rant and rave and claim Jerusalem as their home, period—never mind the facts. They conveniently choose to ignore that others have strong claims too, and that those claims have nothing to do with European imperialism.

While a detailed account of the Arab League's political reshuffling and its anti-Israeli rhetoric are outside the scope of this prophetically-inclined work on Iran, it is worth noting that Iran's emergence in 1935 as Iran, the modern nation-state, happened at a time when Arab powers were bent on asserting sovereignty against the "occidental" "West" as well as over their respective "oriental" constituents[8]—those "constituents" being a variety of very good-hearted and -natured Arabic people, located in their respective geographical locations.[9] That these new powers were particularly intent on distancing themselves from European influences is telling, for fiercely independent rule and anti-Western rhetoric are still vociferously woven into the tapestry of Islamic verbiage, with

---

8 "Occidental" refers to the "West" while "Oriental" means "East." Though the terms have seemingly fallen out of usage in America, they are still used in Europe to denote the respective cultures.

9 I note this here given my *not* wanting to sound like I am discriminating against Arab peoples, many of whom are good people—as far as it goes with the best of people's natures generally. Of concern particularly are the "regional spiritual powers," and the spiritual forces behind them driving them. (See Eph. 6:12.)

no signs of the anti-Western attitudes and consequentially harsh language abating any time soon.

While Islamic nation-states are given to distancing themselves from European influences in their rhetoric, other equally dutiful Muslims seem bent on penetrating into European culture in their reality; and these, as we shall see, may prove to be the more threatening at day's end.

Writing "European Not Christian," in the 30 May 2005 edition of the *U. S. News & World Report*, Jay Tolson noted that there were 1,000,000 Muslims in Europe in 1945, whereas there were 18,000,000 residing there in 2005. This is a marked increase just 60 years later, don't you think? With Turkey's entrance into the European Union, Tolson adds another 62,000,000 Muslims and wonders if 80,000,000 Muslims in a more broadly reconstituted Europe might have an effect on Europe's identity in the near future. Might it be that moderate Muslims will be more influential in reshaping Christian culture than radical Muslims? Tolson seems to think that it will—as do I—given Europe's declining interest in biblical Christianity.

According to the Pew Research Center, only 11% of the French claim that religion is important to them, followed by 21% of Germans and then 33% of Britons. Never mind the radical Muslims for the moment, moderate Muslims by contrast—in Europe, as elsewhere—are disposed to place great stock in their religion and may well yield greater influence over time. Bat Ye'or, whose writings focus predominantly on the history of non-Muslims under Muslim rule, concurs. Interviewed by Adi Schwartz in the Israeli paper *Haaretz*, she warns: "If it keeps on this way, Europe will become a vassal, a satellite of the Arab world, which is larger in terms of numbers."[10]

Islam's steady incline, coupled with Christianity's marked decline, is arguably a recipe for Western cultural disintegration and Islamic integration, is it not?[11] So it would seem. Book titles being published with titles like *EuroArabia* and *Londonistan* explore and lament the alarming trend toward the Islamization of Europe. The ever-increasing Islamic presence, as

---

[10] Culled from *Haaretz* (June 20, 2006), p. 7.

[11] Might Christian culture (or portions of it) be on a "fast track" to annihilation? If so, will Christian Europeans eventually be forced to submit to authoritarian, Islamic ways, along with the totalitarian governments which evolve out of Islamic worldviews? Will Christian culture succumb to an Islamic vision, replete with redefined philosophy, government, religion and more? Should Christians go quietly into the darkness, and toward an eventual cultural and philosophical slaughter? Those who are lethargic and indifferent in the face of Christianity's marked decline—as most are—say "yes" by their silence, if not by their intentions. By good men and women remaining silent, they contribute toward Europe's retooling, and invite changes in Western approaches to education, social integration, art, architecture, literature and government, not to mention religion. If, however, some are minded to rouse themselves, one still wonders the following: What is one to do? What is Europe's hope? In the Middle Ages, soldiers bravely withstood hordes of bellicose Muslim invaders bent on securing and transforming the continent by the dint of their dogged determination. What sort of army can Christian Europe marshal now? Study groups!? Should Eurocentric scholars get together, scrutinize the problem and write hard-to-read books on the subject? While there may indeed be some value in this, one still wonders whether sage analysis, itself, would create sufficient energy to rouse Europeans and prompt some to throw off indifference and reverse the declining situation. What is the hope of Christian Europe? Writing in the August 2005 edition of the Christ for the Nations magazine, under the title "European Identity Shifting," Freda Lindsay posits that "the [singular] remedy" for the wholesale abandonment of Christianity and the eventual destruction of Christian culture "is a Holy Spirit revival" (p. 12). Freda is correct, is she not?

we shall see, may well have significant prophetic and apocalyptic implications—ones that are particularly related to Iran and the coming battle of Armageddon.

Having briefly introduced Iran in history, I will offer now a brief treatment of Iran in prophecy. Believing that it's best to begin with familiar sources before venturing into unfamiliar ones, I'll start by recalling some commonly employed New Testament apocalyptic texts, after which we will devote special attention to the "Armageddon" text in the New Testament. A subsequent chapter will explore Iran in other ancient Jewish sources.

Introducing Iran in Prophecy

In response to the question "What will be the sign of your coming and of the end of the age?" (Mt. 24:3), Jesus (called "Yeshua" by Jews) informed His Israeli Jewish followers that "deception" will abound at day's end (4-5) and that "wars and rumors of wars" will cause angst for many in the region (6)—and the world. Though He predicted various "nations rising against nations" (7), the biblical narrative pays special attention to one particular nation— *Israel*—when He decrees war, culminating at the climactic Battle of Armageddon played out to the north, then moving southward to Jerusalem proper. This is particularly noted, as is the observation that the Savior (Yeshua!) will one day return to Jerusalem, with Judeans on hand saying, "Blessed is He who comes in the Name of the Lord" (Mt. 23:39).

The Savior's jubilant and triumphal arrival in Jerusalem comes on the heels of a major conflict. Zechariah the prophet reports this in Chapter 12: "I will make Jerusalem a cup of drunkenness to all the surrounding peoples, when they lay siege against Judah and Jerusalem" at day's end (2). The enemies will "devour all the surrounding peoples on the right hand and on the left…but Jerusalem shall be inhabited again in her own place—Jerusalem" (6b). Verse 7 declares that "the Lord will save the tents of Judah first…" during the war. Verses 8 and 9 go on to foretell that "In that day the Lord will defend the inhabitants of Jerusalem…and seek to destroy all the nations that come against Jerusalem," resulting in (11) "as great a mourning as…in the plain of Megiddon" —as with the infamous "Armageddon" battle.

We have seen the coming war and Armageddon's place in it; now let's consider how Iran fits into this climactic scenario—one described by both Yeshua (Jesus) and Zechariah. The famous Armageddon text in *Revelation* is reproduced below, followed by the famous "Second Coming" text. I will reflect upon each briefly, paying special attention to Iran's place in the Armageddon story.

> Rev. 16:12 Then the sixth angel poured out his bowl on the great river Euphrates, and its water was dried up, so that the way of the kings of the East might be prepared. 13 And I saw three unclean spirits like frogs, coming out of the mouth of the dragon, out of the mouth of the beast, and out of the mouth of the false prophet. 14 For they are spirits of demons, performing signs, which go out to the kings of the earth and of the whole world, to gather them to the battle of the great day of God Almighty. 15 "Behold I am coming as a thief. Blessed is he who watches, and keeps his garments, lest he walk naked and they see his shame." 16 And they gathered them together to the place in Hebrew, "Armageddon."

Simply put, one can gather from this passage that (1) the Euphrates River will dry up, and that its doing so will (2) open a pathway for innumerable multitudes of blood-lusty and frenzied masses to assemble for a climactic showdown where (3) the long-anticipated conflagration will be played out on "the Great Day of God Almighty" at a place called (4) Armageddon. After noting from where the Evil One makes his entrance—from the region just east of the Euphrates (from Iran!)—the Apostle John later noted the "King of Kings's" arrival into the conflict:

> Rev. 19:11 Now I saw heaven opened, and behold, a white horse and He who sat on him was Faithful and True, and in righteousness He judges and makes war. 12 His eyes were a flame of fire, and on His head were many crowns, He had a name written that no one knew except Himself. 13 He was clothed with a robe dipped in blood, and His name is called the Word of God. 14 And the armies of heaven, clothed in fine linen, white and clean, followed Him on white horses. 15 Now out of His mouth goes a sharp sword, that, with it, He should strike the nations. And He Himself will rule them with a rod of iron. He Himself treads the winepress of the fierceness and wrath of Almighty God. 16 And He has on His robe and on His thigh a name written: 'King of Kings and Lord of Lords.'

> 19:17 Then I saw an angel standing in the sun; and he cried with a loud voice, saying to all the birds that fly in the midst of heaven, 'Come and gather together for the supper of the great God, 18 that you may eat the flesh of kings, the flesh of captains, the flesh of the mighty men, the flesh of horses and of those who sit on them, and the flesh of all the people, free and slave, both small and great.' 19 And I saw the beast, the kings of the earth, and their armies, gathered together to make war against Him who sat on the horse and against His army. 20 Then the beast was captured, and with him the false prophet who worked signs in his presence, by which he deceived those

> who received the mark of the beast and those who worshipped his image. These two were cast alive into the lake of fire burning with brimstone. 21 And the rest were killed with the sword which proceeded from the mouth of Him who sat on the horse. And all the birds were filled with their flesh.
>
> 20:1 Then I saw an angel coming down from heaven, having the key to the bottomless pit and a great chain in his hand. 2 He had laid hold of the dragon, that serpent of old, who is the Devil and Satan, and bound him for a thousand years; 3 and he cast him into the bottomless pit....

Revelation 19:11 observes the arrival of One upon a white horse who comes to judge and make war against the evil one. In verse 14 "armies of heaven," likewise on "white horses," enter the battle with Him. Referred to in verse 16 as "King of Kings and Lord of Lords," this ruler "strikes the nations and...treads the winepress of the fierceness and wrath of Almighty God." (15) John then sees an angel beckoning hungry vultures to come and celebrate "the supper of the great God." (17). What he has in mind in this interesting feast (!?) is their consuming "the flesh of kings, the flesh of captains, the flesh of the mighty men, the flesh of horses and of those who sit on them, and the flesh of all the people, free and slave, both small and great" (18), a description of the land littered with corpses as a result of the battle royal. God emerges victorious, we're told in verse 20: "the beast was captured and with him the false prophet who worked signs in his presence, by which he deceived those who received the mark of the beast and those who worshipped his image. These two were cast alive into the lake of fire burning with brimstone." In verse 21, "the rest were killed with the sword which proceeded from the mouth of Him who sat on the horse. And all the birds were filled with their flesh." The riveting story then wraps up with the victorious king thrusting the evil one into the bottomless pit, in chapter 20. There, in verse 2, He "lays hold of the dragon, that serpent of old, who is the Devil and Satan, and binds him for a thousand years," after which He casts him into the bottomless pit and seals it shut (3a).

Apocalyptic language will be considered in some detail elsewhere in this volume, with particular attention given to the apocalyptic images employed in ancient Jewish writings. We've been looking at the preceding Scripture simply to note that *the doorway to the final Armageddon conflict is opened at the Euphrates*, from whence the wicked "kings of the east" make their crossing and entrance, setting in motion the countdown to "Armageddon." It seems prudent to bring this up in a preliminary discussion of Islamic growth in general, and of emergent Iranian activity in particular; for, those who consult a map—any map!—to learn the name of the country just to the east of the Euphrates River will un-mistakenly confront the modern nation-state of "Iran." For this reason, especially if taken literally, *one is forced to conclude that Iran has a part to play in history's most infamous conflagration, the dreaded End Time drama known as the "Battle of Armageddon."*

On the twentieth anniversary of the modern Iranian revolution, Ayatolla Khamenei reminded his constituents that the "irreconcilable enmity [with Iran] was the American government and its Zionist appendix [Israel] in the Middle East." This remains the country's official position. Given that Iran's current president President Mahmoud Ahmadinejad sounds much the same, and with the country's escalating and ever-threatening nuclear capabilities becoming a factor, I thought it worthwhile to pursue the Iran-Armageddon connection and present my findings to you.

With John the Apostle's revelatory words reverberating in our ears, I posit that truth-loving prophecy students should pay attention to Iranian rhetoric and influence. The important part that Iran played in biblical history—albeit under other names—and the anticipated role that Iran will apparently be playing in the future are good reasons for biblical students to calmly[12] take stock of what's happening today, and consider discernable patterns[13] connected to Iran's taking the lead in expressing Arab, anti-Israeli rhetoric.

Summary

So, what have you gleaned from this book so far? If I've been successful, you join me in believing that the Iran-Revelation connection is at least worth exploring—particularly because

---

[12] I don't want to overplay my hand at the start, and so I will intentionally tone down my own rhetoric. Though I do want my readers to see the importance of my thesis, I want to avoid startling some in the interest of drawing individuals into my narrative. As for "turning up" the rhetoric, I believe that there is a time and place for "sounding the trumpet" and for "beating the battle drums"—even in this book; this, however, is neither the time nor the place in the volume—at least, not just yet. There is a place for the canon firings in the "1812 Overture"; but it is slated for the end of the symphonic piece, and not the beginning. Thus reminded, to better serve you, I want to move us away from the fascinating world of biblical prophecy, to first take you to the more pedestrian-sounding, blander world of history—biblical history, particularly. I hope you'll forgive me for so doing. I realize that not everyone loves history. Still, by so doing, I will show you how the land of Iran—known as "Parthia" in the New Testament era, and as "Persia" to those at the end of the Old Testament era—has always been a major player in biblical events.

[13] If you walk through a pine forest and run into a single Redwood tree you may say, "My, that's a freak accident." If you run into another one shortly thereafter, you will likely say: "My, what a coincidence." If you run into yet another one, you may well say: "Goodness, this is a pattern!" I note this here to underscore that there is a discernable pattern, an historical one that has interesting implications for the interpretation of prophecy. Whether this proves true for you is up to you, and will be determined by you later.

Iran is noted as being the doorway to Armageddon. In addition, you've heard the Apostle John directly (in Revelation), much as you have heard from the deceased Iranian "Ayatolla" and, to a lesser degree, the present Iranian president. Mindful of these voices, let us now dig deeper still and go to the first century Judean world where we'll consider what others have said about ancient Iran and how an Iranian Empire was construed by them to factor into end-of-time events in a way that effects both Western and Israeli cultures. On to biblical history in Chapter 2, The *Place.*

II

The *Place of* the Iranian-Armageddon Connection in Ancient Jewish and Roman Histories

Iran in Ancient Roman History

Writing in *Backgrounds to Early Christianity*, Dr. Everett Ferguson noted that between 250 and 227BC, "with the gradual establish-ment of the Greco-Bactrian and Parthian kingdoms, everything east of Media was lost,"[1] meaning that little is known of Parthia's history till its absorption into the Seleucid Empire following Alexander the Great's well-attested conquests. Parthia's first ruler is known to have been Arsaces I, who revolted against the Bactrian Greeks and fled, eventually securing a foothold south of the Caspian Sea where he set up his rule. Later, expansionist Parthian kings like Mithradates I (171-138BC) and Artabanus II (128-124BC) got the better of peoples in the Iranian plateau and the Tigris-Euphrates Valley, both of which came under Parthian sway where they remained till Parthia was militarily bested by Ardashir, King of the Sasanians in 224AD. Prior to its fall, ancient Parthia/Iran was known for having amassed great

[1] Everett Ferguson, *Backgrounds to Early Christianity* (Grand Rapids: Eerdmans, 1993), p. 18

wealth through maintaining tight control over trade routes between Asia and the broadly constituted Greco-Roman empire, for keeping Rome "in check" by halting its visions of eastward expansion, and for playing host to multitudes of Jews. In this regard, Dr. Ferguson went on to note that by the first century AD "the Jews were numerous, spread widely over the Roman Empire and even outside it, especially in the Parthian Empire."[2] The Jewish presence in Parthia/Iran becomes significant, as we shall see later; for now, let's be content to note this, but investigate Roman relationship more directly.

In his *Lives of the Noble Greeks and Romans*, the ancient moralist and biographer Plutarch told the story of western Rome's interactions with the militant, eastern Parthians. On one occasion, the wealthiest man in ancient Rome lost his life in an ill-fated campaign against the Parthians, during which an enormous number of "crack" Roman Legions were annihilated by them—perhaps Rome's worst military disaster in its lengthy history. Rome's crushing defeat by the Iranian/Parthians arguably became the linguistic model for the telling of Rome's final judgment and demise; for that matter, it may partly explain why Iran/Parthia's predicted invasion of the west at the "end of days," factors into ancient prophecy in Revelation, as elsewhere. We'll get to the prophetic side later; for now, let's attend to the history.

Here's the story of Western civilization's first clash with the Eastern Parthians.

Marcus Licinius Crassus Dives, known simply as "Crassus," was one of Rome's wealthiest citizens, said to even own much of the property in the city of Rome itself. Disconcerted by the

---

[2] Ibid., p. 580.

"Slave Revolt" under Spartacus in 74BC, this rich man decided to get the better of Rome's runaway property (its slaves), and was immensely successful in his endeavors.

Gladiators and escaped slaves amassed and holed up with Spartacus by Mount Vesuvius. After Spartacus' band initially defeated two legionary cohorts (numbering 400-600 men each), approximately 70,000 slaves joined "the rebellion," a number that eventually surpassed 100,000. With "deep pockets," Crassus raised and funded six new Roman Legions, himself. He eventually trapped Spartacus and successfully "put down" the revolt. As punishment, he had 6,000 of the surviving slave-rebels crucified along the Apian Way, lining the road from Capua to Rome. In the wake of his successful exploits, and owing to his financial influence, Crassus was granted joint rule with Gnaeus "Pompeius" Magnes and Gaius "Julius Caesar"—known respectively to us as "Pompei" and "Julius Caesar."

Though Crassus' victory over slaves was not seen as being on par with Pompei's and Julius Caesar's victories over "real armies," Romans, nevertheless, felt indebted to Crassus and, in response, established a "triumvirate"—a tenuous arrangement whereby the three celebrated warrior-leaders shared power. Feeling eclipsed by the other leaders' growing military fame and glory, the restless Crassus longed for another, more credible win, by which he could commend himself to the Romans once again, and be considered by them as being on par with the other two legends sharing power with him.

An opportunity finally presented itself.

After being granted a proconsular command in Syria, Crassus set about to raise a new army, with which he intended to conquer Iran/Parthia. He wanted to use Syria as a staging area in a major war against the Parthians to the east—a war that would bring him the military glory that Julius Caesar and Pompei enjoyed and that he so greatly coveted. Forces at his personal command eventually topped 35,000 infantry (about seven Legions) and 4,000 cavalry. Joined the following year by his son Publius (who had been a Legate in the service of Julius Caesar) and 1,000 of his cavalry, Crassus felt "in the ready" and made his move eastward.

When Crassus first crossed the Euphrates from the west, a number of Greek populations immediately came to his side, a move that intoxicated him with premature enthusiasm—and prompted him to foolishly drop his guard. The Armenian Artavasdes II brought an additional 6,000 horsemen and 30,000 infantry for the Parthian war; but the better part were eventually deployed elsewhere, and were of no direct use to Crassus, who would desperately need them soon. Overly confident as he was, Crassus was succored into an ill-fated battle at Carrhae, being fooled by an Arab (Nabatean) chieftan named Ariamnes, himself nothing more than an Iranian/Parthian spy.

In 53BC, at Carrhae, the Parthians drew Crassus into a trap, out-maneuvered him, and squarely defeated his forces. In the process, they gave Rome one of the most humiliating military defeats in its illustrious history: 20,000 Roman foot soldiers lost their lives in the debacle, 10,000 were captured and subsequently sold into slavery. Even greedy Crassus, himself, was caught and slain shortly thereafter. Not a particularly good day for the Romans, to be sure.

Writing in the late second, early third century, historian Dio Cassius—not to be confused with Crassus—reported that when Crassus' body was sent to the Parthian King Orodes II, molten gold was poured down the throat of Crassus' corpse, an inglorious punishment for the insatiable avarice of a man who wanted more and more and simply could not be satisfied. Never mind Crassus' arrogance; worse yet for Roman state pride, the Legions' coveted military standards were captured and kept by the Parthians. For these and other reasons, Rome wanted revenge; but at that time it simply didn't have the time or the resources to exact it. Preoccupied with other pressing issues on Rome's western fronts, they ignored the situation with Parthia in the east for the better part of 30 years. It wasn't until 20BC—some 33 years later—that "Caesar Augustus" (Octavian) secured the Legions' standards' release from the Parthians and brought them back to Rome where they were stored in the temple of Mars. After that, Parthia's re-emergence in the constellation of Roman concerns was hastened by Parthia's meddling in the affairs of one of Rome's recent holdings—the ancient province of Judea.

Iran in Ancient Jewish History

We turn now to first-century Judean history, deemed an important prelude to prophecy, and connect it to our developing Parthian/Iranian story, after which the story will string together like pearls on a necklace, with prophecy added later.

Before being annexed as a colony at the eastern end of the ancient Roman Empire, Judea was considered one of Alexander the Great's Greek holdings, after which it was passed to King Antiochus, who operated out of Syria. Though Judea fought for and subsequently won a brief season of relative autonomy from foreign domination, the Jewish nation-state eventually became a Roman satellite in the first century BC and was managed accordingly, to the chagrin of many. Though the full story of Judean and Roman political intrigue goes beyond the scope of this book, it is worth noting that the Jewish province had been administratively divided by the Roman overlords equally between two sons of Antipater, whom Rome favored as its Judean ruler: Phasael and Herod. Both sons were referred to by the Romans as "Tetrarchs."[3] Over time, Rome established itself in Judea; and after a period of time, the Romans placed the Herodians as their representatives to attend to their interests.

Not long thereafter, Parthia in the east moved westward and invaded the Roman province of Judea, killing Phasael the Tetrarch, which left Herod alone and woefully unprotected. The emboldened and powerful Iranian/Parthians placed their puppet Antigonus in power in Judea, believing him to have a better claim to the throne than Herod. Much to Herod's chagrin, for three years the Parthian pawn Antigonus held the titles of "King" and "High Priest" over Judea—but not for long.

Not the least bit pleased by his diminished lot in the "turn of affairs" in and around Judea, Herod fled westward. En route, he dropped off his immediate family members at the Masada fortress, made haste to Cleopatra in Egypt, and eventually went off to Rome to secure official support against the Parthians.

With no love for the Parthians themselves (for reasons previously noted), and wanting a stable buffer against their eastern rivals in Parthia, the Roman Senate was quite pleased to support Herod in his bid for the throne. Thus, when he appealed to the Senate in 40BC, he was swiftly and unanimously

---

[3] An inferior term denoting one who exercised sway over part of a province, no more.

appointed as the Romans' choice for "King"[4] in Judea. *Worth noting by New Testament students: "Herod the Great" (34-4BC), so called, was given indisputable power over all Judea on the heels of a threatening Parthian/Iranian invasion*, to give Rome a loyal puppet kingdom on their eastern front to, among other things, stave off Iranian/Parthian advances.

It is interesting to note for our purposes that, just prior to the dawning of the Christian era, Western powers (Rome) were enmeshed with Israeli powers (the newly constituted Judean province) in a bid to secure both Israeli and Western cultures against Parthian/Iranian aggression from the east. Is this not comparable to the current situation, where Western powers see a successful, modern Israeli nation-state as a buffer supporting Western interests in and around the region?

The story of Western Europeans in conflict with Eastern Arabians, with Israel in the middle, goes back to the time of Jesus. Reminders in the book *Revelation* that, at "day's end," forces from the East cross the Euphrates and come to battle at Armageddon suggest that the story has eschatological significance. Before getting to this focal concern of the book, I want to pull back and fill in the background.

Let us look at first-century author Josephus' firsthand account of Iranian-Western tensions and the fact that *the ancients believed that the historical Parthian Invasion was, itself, a precursor to a climactic battle between Western and Eastern Arabian cultures, with Israel drawn into the middle.* How this dovetails with Old and New Testament prophecy, and how it has possible bearing upon the emergence of Iran as a nation-state today, will be considered later. As noted, first I want to consider Josephus' firsthand accounting of the above.

---

[4] Everett Ferguson, *Backgrounds to Early Christianity*, p. 389.

Writing under "Herod's Predecessors," the first century writer Flavious Josephus was not the least bit sheepish about negatively describing greedy Crassus' failed campaign against the Parthians, which we just examined. After relating that Crassus "took over the governorship of Syria,"[5] Josephus immediately notes that for "the campaign against the Parthians, he [maliciously] removed all the gold from the Sanctuary in Jerusalem, including the 2,000 talents that Pompey had not touched." Not particularly intimidated by the bellicose Romans, "the Parthians swept forward," Josephus tells us, "… but were driven back by Crassus... [who later] went back to the Euphrates to prevent a Parthian crossing"[6]—at least for the time being.

Josephus goes on to inform that "Barzapharnes, the Parthian [/Iranian] satrap" was "persuaded" to "bring back Antigonus [of Hasmonean descent], and make him King"[7] of Judea—over and against the Roman "Tetrarch," Herod. Displeased by Rome's favoring of Herod and preferring the Parthian choice, "Jews flocked to Antigonus' standard," and a battle ensued in Jerusalem proper, during which the rabble supporting Antigonus was herded into the Jerusalem Temple, ending in a stalemate.

"Now came the Feast of Pentecost," reports Josephus, "and all the vicinity of the Temple—in fact, the whole city—was filled with people from the countryside, most of them armed."[8] The winds of war were blowing!

---

5 *The Jewish War*, pp. 50-51 (I, 172-187).
6 Ibid., p. 51 (I, 187).
7 Ibid., p. 60 (I, 245).
8 Ibid.

Wanting to bring the conflict to an end and restore order, an allegedly unbiased intermediary was brought in to mediate—a Parthian/Iranian named Pacorus: The sneaky "Pacorus," says Josephus, "had come avowedly to end the strife, but in reality to assist Antigonus."[9] This he did by brokering a deal involving the gifting of 500 women "to Parthian use" along with "1,000 talents." The stealthy scheme succeeded: Phasael lost his power and his life; Herod's authority was greatly diminished; and the Parthian puppet, Antigonus, was enthroned.

Making haste to get redress for his grievances, as noted previously Herod fled westward and regrouped. Josephus' account reads as follows: "The Parthians, learning what had happened, went in pursuit [of Herod... who] finally made a dash for Masada."[10] "[L]eaving eight hundred men there to protect the women, with provisions sufficient for a siege, he hurried on to Petra in Arabia."[11] With Herod on the run, Josephus says that "the Parthians in Jerusalem turned to looting"[12] and that "Parthian conduct became so outrageous that they filled the whole country with war to the death."[13]

Iranian/Parthians were at odds with Rome, much as they invoked the ire of some Judeans by meddling in Israeli affairs. In response, Herod first appealed to local Arabs for assistance; they, however, were not kindly disposed toward him: "Meeting with the hostility of the Arabs," says Josephus, Herod "turned toward Egypt,"[14] where "he received a splendid welcome from Cleopatra, who hoped to employ him

---

[9] Ibid., p. 61 (I, 261).
[10] Ibid., p. 62 (I, 261).
[11] Ibid.
[12] Ibid.
[13] Ibid, p. 63 (I, 276).
[14] Ibid.

as a commander in a projected campaign."[15] He avoided her, however, and "sailed for Rome,"[16] to make his troubles known to Antony, Caesar's second in command.

"Antony," we're told, "was very grieved… [and] decided on the spot that the man he had once made Tetrarch should now be the king of the Jews."[17] Considering the puppet king installed by the Parthians to be a threat, Antony "convened the Senate" immediately[18] and disavowed the disobedient Iranian-placed Judean puppet king Antigonus, who "had now accepted the crown from the Parthians in defiance of the Romans."[19] Josephus tells us that "These revelations angered the Senate, and when Antony rose to suggest that the Parthian war was an added reason for making Herod king, they all voted in favour.[20] The House adjourned, and Antony and Caesar went out with Herod between them, the consuls and other magistrates leading the way in order to offer sacrifice and to deposit the decree in the Capitol."[21]

Writing later under "Herod Master of Palestine" (sic.[22]), and while noting Herod's war, Josephus mentions "Ventidius sending for Silo and Herod to take part in the Parthian war."[23] Some time later, however, when the Parthians were "driven out,"[24] at Antony's behest Ventidius "sent support to

---

15 Ibid., p. 64 (I, 276).
16 Ibid.
17 Ibid.
18 Ibid., p. 65 (I, 285).
19 Ibid.
20 This is the British spelling: favour instead of favor.
21 Op. Cit., p. 65. (I, 285).
22 An abbreviation noting an error. The land should be referred to as Israel/Judea and not Palestine.
23 Ibid., p. 69 (I, 315).
24 Ibid., p. 70 (I, 315).

Herod" in order to secure his position against Antigonus.[25] Later on, after Antony secured Cleopatra's cooperation, "she [even] escorted Antony as far as the Euphrates on his way to fight the Parthians,"[26] after which "she persuaded Antony to entrust Herod with the war against [the] Arabs."[27] Josephus goes on to inform us that Herod's "nephew was later killed by the Parthians,"[28] after which he eventually reminds readers that "Herod's brother died at the hands of the Parthians,"[29] too. In a chapter entitled "War Clouds"—where taunts against the rebellious Judeans are noted—Josephus describes the Parthian/Iranians, along with the Thracians, Gauls, Spaniards, Germanic peoples and Britons. There he ably reflects Roman sentiment, referring to the Parthians as "*the most warlike race of all*, rulers of so many nations and protected by such vast forces."[30]

Might this assessment contribute toward an understanding of John's vision that masses from present-day Iran/Parthia will converge for the world's worst war, Armageddon? Perhaps. In either case, it does help us realize that ancient Romans construed themselves as being trapped in an uncertain world, one in which they found it necessary to marshal resources to deal with forces round about them.

Josephus' ancient historical writings reveal that, in order to thwart Parthian military intrusion and political intrigue, the Roman Senate was pressed to install Herod the Great as king over Judea. Rome hoped to secure its eastern flank against

---

25 Ibid.

26 Ibid., p. 75 (I, 363).

27 Ibid., p. 76 (I, 363).

28 Ibid., 93 (I, 490).

29 Ibid., p. 125. (II, 54). The reference to "brother," of course, is to Phasael, who was mentioned previously.

30 Ibid., p. 160 (II, 377).

the advances of the barbarian Parthians, deeming them to be the "most warlike race of all" and a horribly uncouth people "protected by such vast forces."[31] The Roman mind had other ways of dealing with life's uncertainties, as we shall see.

Summary

For a variety of reasons, many ancient Romans and Jews alike were vexed by Iranian/Parthian intrusions. What would they do? What could they do to hold the powerful Parthians at bay? Tensions created by the west-east struggle with Parthia facilitated a variety of responses — some political, some religious. With the political ones noted above, we'll proceed to attend to the spiritual ones in the following chapter. Therein, and after a brief consideration of how ancient pagans and Jews alike viewed prophecy, a variety of prophetic texts relevant to Iran, Israel, and the Middle East will be brought into the conversation more directly.

---

[31] As noted above, the aforementioned assessment forces both the observation and conclusion that, as the Christian era was dawning over Jerusalem, Western civilization was itself enmeshed with Israeli powers in a bid to secure both Israel itself and Western culture from the advances of Parthian/Iranian aggression—as is the case today. Personally, I find the historical Iranian/Parthian intrusion into Israeli and Western affairs to be quite interesting, especially in light of modern circumstances and ancient biblical prophecies that will be considered later.

III

The *Space for* the Iranian-Armageddon Connection in Ancient Apocalyptic Literature

Introduction

Ancient Romans appreciated prophetic oracles as did ancient Jews, both of whom were yearning for Divine assistance in their precarious worlds.[1] Because Jews mourned their relative loss of power and autonomy, disdained their absorption into

[1] If one will permit a play on words, one can observe that in antiquity both Jews and pagans had something in common: both were occupied with "right"/"rite." "Right," of course, speaks of moral correctness, and is of paramount importance to Jews. "Rite" speaks of ceremony and liturgy: and rites were of primary importance to ancient Greeks and Romans who were, themselves, devoutly religious, but who were inclined to be so without the moral underpinnings of "rightness," so important to Jesus, Paul and their Jewish counterparts. Pharisees in Paul's day were more concerned with what was "right"; Sadducees—inhabiting and managing the priestly, Temple guilds—were, by contrast, seemingly more interested in ceremonial "rites," though moral rightness figured, too. Some Christian traditions emphasize "rites" (stylized liturgical services, etc.) and moral "rightness"; some place more emphasis on one or the other. Romans, by way of contrast, were not nearly as morally inclined, though they demonstrated interest in prophetic omens and showed a fondness for superstitious, ceremonial rites.

the pagan Roman Empire, and kept mindful of biblical promises that a Messianic and Davidic leader would one day arise and lead Israel to victory over and away from the godless heathen, many ancient Jews restlessly looked upward to God and outward toward an uncertain future. They looked to Heaven for answers to earthly problems, and anxiously awaited the tangible manifestation of His will and ways through Scripture study, through the fulfillment of prophetic predictions, and through searching out God's hand in their evolving circumstances. They made space in their thinking for prophetic fulfillments.

In similar ways, morally-rudderless Romans envisioned a cosmogony (a creation story) wherein mortal humans were depicted as trapped in an unfriendly and uncharted, supernaturally-driven and mysterious universe, one that came replete with myriad, unseen forces: some good, some inhospitable and potentially hazardous. Though they did not agree with Jews on what or who the "Divine" was, both deemed Divine help imperative to ward off the evil spirits and to secure their footholds in this world.

Jews had Torah observance, with instruction of its particulars dispensed in and through local synagogues. Jews had occasional Temple participation and daily prayers by which they transcended their quagmires. As a defense against the prevailing spiritual and material uncertainty, the Roman mind was given both to the employment of religious rituals and the deployment of prophecies. From the Romans' perspective, religion helped them to secure the favor and protection of their gods[2] from inhospitable forces deemed a threat—from Iranian/Parthian threats, for example.

---

2 Known as Zeus to the Greeks, and as Jupiter to the Romans, the heavenly father of the gods presided over the association of Olympian

Treatments of Hebrew prophecy follow. To help explain both the Roman acceptance and desirability of prophetic impulses, a brief introduction of Roman religious sensibilities and practices seems in order. This will be the object of my attention now.

---

divines, and was the patriarch of the famous ancient Greek religious pantheon. Because—like man—no god should be alone, a godly wife was needed: enter Hera, (Juno to the Romans). She was the wife of the patriarch and came to be appropriately associated with marriage and women. Unfortunately, as is the case with some mere mortals, the divine Zeus had a problem with his wandering libido—with adultery. Sexual encounters with mortal women later invoked the ire of his chagrined wife—but more on that later. Other royal family members included his brother, Poseidon (the Romans' Neptune). He was the god of the seas. Athena (Minerva to the Romans), was Zeus' daughter. She was the virgin goddess of wisdom, of the arts and was herself personally the protector of Athens. Military motifs are associated with her, and she was said to have sprung from Zeus' head, at birth, both fully grown and fully armed. Apollo was distinguished among many as the "all Greek" god/lad, the idealized Greek male, known for manly beauty, music, archery, prophecy, medicine, flocks and herds, law, civilization and more—these being staples of refined culture. Apollo embodied the characteristics that brought the Greeks pride. He had a twin sister—Artemis (Diana)—the chaste goddess of the countryside, involved as a goddess in childbirth. She may have been chaste in Greek mythology; others in the family, however, were not so inclined: unbridled licentiousness and jealousy seemed more the order of the day—even among the Olympian divines. In fact, it was the Greek acceptance and celebration of immodesty and sexual impropriety that prompted Torah-observant Jews to disdain and condemn Hellenistic culture outright. Both the Greeks and the Romans who worshipped the Olympian divines placed a premium on militancy and worshipped the gods of war. Ares (Mars) was the god of war. Because courageous soldiers needed pleasure too, they worshiped the god of wine, Dionysus (Bacchus)—of which more will be said in a few moments. Hephaestus (Vulcan) was the god of fire and crafts, a manufacturing deity. Lastly, Hermes (Mercury) was the messenger of the gods, in addition to which he guarded roadways, and even conducted souls to Hades—to the frightening abyss in the Greek underworld.

The means by which Romans, whose empire overlapped Greece, sought to hear from and please their militant, lusty and emotionally unstable Greek gods is varied.[3] Believing that folk could placate the divines and secure benefits for themselves as a result, ancient Romans frequented temples where they brought offerings. Greek, and then Roman, temples even had treasury rooms to hold the gifts offered to the deities in the interest of securing their fancy on Olympus and their consequential favors on earth beneath. The faithful came bearing offerings expecting to receive something in exchange—a gift or a sign from the gods, an omen or an oracle.[4]

As superstitious as many apparently were, accessing heaven's powers in some form was deemed important. So prominent was this type of religious activity that cities were known to send official delegations to the sacred shrines to inquire of the divinities' prophets on matters of economics, war, politics, and to address official religious matters. Religious sites were thus perceived as prophecy centers. This was central in ancient Roman pre-Christian belief systems, as well as in Hellenistic Jewish ones; the giving and receiving of oracles should not be construed as merely a marginal phenomenon, but as a widespread practice deemed acceptable to all classes of society.

---

3 A proper burial, for example, was considered very important lest the deceased Roman wander perpetually in a phantasmal, ghost-like, state of un-rest, never being afforded the peace granted to the dead who had been properly interned. The *Iliad* opened with souls being thrust into Hades, which was depicted as a dreary place where, according to Homer, life continued but in a manner not worth living. How might one avoid this dread non-existence? Roman religious tradition attained special importance owing to a belief that it could purchase safe passage to the next world, much as it could enhance the passage through this one.

4 Collins noted that "in general, they were consulted in serious crisis of any kind" (Ibid, p.320).

Though there were a variety of different "daughter" sanctuaries in the ancient Roman world, pride of place was given to the religious "mother house" at Delphi—what was considered to have been Zeus' main spot and the actual "center of the earth." It was at this site, supposedly, that Apollo, the quintessential Greek male and warrior, once killed the "Python"—a spectacular she-serpent, deemed sacred to a certain earth goddess in early Minoan (Bronze Age Crete) civilization. For this reason, the heroic and idealized Apollo featured significantly at Delphi, where he was perceived as Zeus' personal representative. It was at Delphi where Apollo is said to have become the actual god of prophecy and the official spokesman for Zeus. A priestess seemed to have been the main feature at the shrines, however, where she presided over the main religious attraction there: that of oracle-giving. At Delphi, Romans solicited the services of a celibate priestess: forgoing sexual activity was construed as a prerequisite to the religious service of uttering prophetic words.[5]

---

[5] The adoration of the wine god Dionysus (Bacchus to the Romans) came replete with mystical and ecstatic celebrations. Wild swirling and dancing was employed through which celebrants worked themselves into a frenzied condition, accompanied by escalated states of emotional and intellectual delirium. It is said that devotion to Dionysus first appealed to women; in time, however, men were brought into the cult. Why the religious abandon? What was the appeal? If "a picture is worth a thousand words," one might do well to consider artwork from the era, a window into the widespread cult. A fresco outside Pompeii in Italy gives us just such a perspective. It pictures a woman defending herself from a powerful, demonic, female figure called a "Dike"—the mythological "goddess of justice." "Dike" has a mind to strike the already beaten and weakened female victim over and again. The miserable victim subjected to the incessant abuse, however, is finally spared the painful experience of relentless judgment, with the result that she, almost entirely naked at this juncture, leaps up in the fresco and swirls about in reckless abandon—an ecstatic response seen as the supposed depiction of a joyous and blissful afterlife, free of all judgment. Bizarre as this story is, the power of frenzy is more amply attested in the adoration of the goddess Atargatis of

How did folk get a personal prophecy? At the temple, a female priestess-prophetess, a "pythia," would go into a trance-like state, from which she would allegedly utter the words of the gods. In such a state, she would be consulted by inquirers who lined up to have an audience with her, given their wanting heavenly affirmation for their respective vexing, earthly concerns. Certain rules were normally imposed upon visitors to the prophetic shrines. An inscription at the temple of Athena at Pergamum reads: "Whoever wishes to visit the temple of the goddess…must refrain from intercourse with

---

Hierapolis in Greece. Wandering priests devoted to Atargatis went about advocating for the cult, and their religious adoration was attended by strange practices, of a sort that dwarfs human imagination. While a donkey carried an image of the goddess in procession, priests moving about in proximity to her image confessed their sins and beat themselves with whips till their blood flowed freely. They danced about in an intoxicated and frenzied state, playing musical instruments all the while. The priests then took up financial offerings, securing alms from among the sympathetic onlookers who were attracted to the odd events. In his *On the Syrian Goddess*, Lucian tells in chapter 51 that, against the backdrop of the loud music and frenzied dance noted above, male priestly candidates would strip off their clothing, grab swords and castrate themselves. They would then run through the city and eventually throw their disconnected organs into a stranger's home, in response to which, they would be granted entrance to the domicile, where they would grab a woman's garment, which would become their new priestly robe. In this way priests joined themselves to the cult of the goddess and wore women's clothing thereafter. The popularization of celibacy for priestesses, of ritual castration among priests, of self-mutilated eunuchs parading about in women's apparel, of naked women sensually dancing about in reckless spiritual abandon, all indicate the marriage between supernatural belief and the bizarre. Judaism, for its part, knew none of this, and condemned it outright. These and other practices, however, were standard fare in Roman culture. Mindful of the above, we shouldn't wonder that Paul had to take up issues related to gender and role confusion, coupled with sexual confusion generally, in his various epistles. Readers cannot understand Paul without understanding his Jewish and Greco-Roman contexts.

his wife (or husband) that day, [and/or] from intercourse with another than his wife (or husband) for the preceding two days." Notice that the temple deity wasn't interested in taking issue with folk having sexual liaisons outside of marriage, for this activity was common amongst their own gods. Having sexual intercourse with "another," be it a male or female, was—in marked contrast to Judaism—not the least bit eschewed. Temporary sexual restraint seemed to be imposed only for purposes of ritual purification. Worth noting, for our purposes (and Paul's), is the fact that Romans would correlate sexual abstinence with divinely inspired prophetic unction: the prophetess, herself, as one may recall, was asexual—a full-time celibate; and her petitioners, for their part, were required to embrace restraint on a part-time basis.[6] Paul took issue with the lack of morality in Roman culture and religion, much as he was given to challenging pagan prophetic types who pestered him every now and again.[7]

---

[6] These insights contribute toward understanding Paul's discussions on human sexuality in some of his correspondences. As with the tendencies prevailing in the culture, some of his religious hearers seemed bent on sexual denial, whereas others seemed bent on sexual indulgence—both impulses of which can be found in Greco-Roman religious experience. Much as conduct at the sacred shrines was regulated, so too was clothing. For example, a woman's hair was to be loose when visiting the temple, and a man's head had to be uncovered. Could these requirements contribute toward our understanding of Paul's notions related to women's hair being a covering in 1 Cor. 11:4-15? Let it simply suffice for now to note that Romans followed various religious rules, being ever so anxious to secure the favor of their various gods.

[7] In Acts 16:16, Luke noted that "a certain slave possessed with a spirit of divination" annoyed Paul and Silas. Luke's Greek text specifically informed that the "possessed" girl who badgered Paul was "possessed of a Pythian spirit." Given that "Pythia" means nothing to most in modern times, the translators simply opted for "spirit of divination," to make the point that the ancient slave was known for being "possessed," and to have been given to the manufacture of "prophetic oracles," or "divination." That the slave-girl's divination-utterances were described as "Pythia" is

The preceding sketch of Roman religion wasn't drawn to legitimize the non-biblical, pagan activities, as much as to impress upon my readers the understanding that *the ancients were interested in prophecies*—Jew and non-Jew alike. With that as a given, we'll now attend to some of what legitimate biblical prophets had to say about their troubled world, after which we will look at some ancient Jewish interpretations of those prophecies.

Prophecies in Jewish Scripture

Introduction

Previously, I noted that I would be using the Jewish Publication Society's Hebrew rendition of prophetic Old Testament texts, and that I would be drawing upon "traditional" Jewish expositors of those texts to inform my readers how Jews interpreted their respective prophecies. On that premise, our primary guide both to and through Isaiah will be Rabbi Dr. I. W. Slotki, (with revisions to his lauded work configured by Rabbi A. J. Rosenberg) as is found in his *Isaiah: Hebrew Text & English Translation with an Introduction and Commentary* (London/New York: Soncino Press, 1983). References to his work noted in my explanations will appear in parentheses with appropriate page numbers following. In like manner, Rabbi S. Fisch (for Ezekiel) will be employed, as will Rabbi Eli Cashdan (for Zechariah), all chosen for the Jewish insights they bring to biblical personalities and subjects in their respective works. I could have expanded my Old Testament texts to include Daniel, Moses' writings, and more;

---

significant, however, given that the cult practice at Delphi was presided over by a celibate prophetess, herself known as a "Pythia." It is thus apparent that the slave-girl in Luke's narrative was at least marginally related to the Delphi cult—as were many. Delphi, in fact, was apparently the "center of gravity" for ancient Roman, prophetic mystical oracle-giving, with other lesser-known sites spread throughout much of the empire, taking their lead from the movement headquartered at Delphi.

I trust, however, that these prophets and interpreters will provide a sufficient introductory accounting for how Jews perceived these prophetic texts.

Isaiah

Though forever mindful of Judah's sinfulness and soon-coming judgment (1:1-5:30), Isaiah nevertheless saw past the abysmal circumstances to the "end of days," when God's will would be manifest by "the Kingdom of God being firmly established" in a restored Judah (Isaiah, p.10). He envisioned Judah's religious triumph with "the recognition of the law of our God by all the nations of the earth" (p.11). Jerusalem is said to be both its spiritual nexus and the "center of world peace," with "the nations streaming to God's house" in response (p.10). Isaiah saw a day when peace would be restored to both the region and the world evidenced by "the abolition of all warfare" (p.10). As evidence of this and more, in 2:2-4 he shared:

> 2:2 And it shall come to pass in the end of days, that the mountain of the Lord's house shall be established as the top of the mountains, and it shall be exalted above the hills; and all nations shall flow unto it. 3 And many peoples shall go and say: "Come ye, let us go up to the mountain of the Lord, to the house of the God of Jacob; and He will teach us His ways, and we will walk in His paths. For out of Zion shall go forth the law and the word of the Lord from Jerusalem. 4 And He will judge between the nations, and shall decide for many peoples; and they shall beat their swords into plowshares, and their spears into pruning hooks; nation shall not lift up sword against nation; neither shall they learn war anymore.

For Isaiah, the long-awaited end to global hostilities comes at "day's end," and is facilitated by an anointed "deliverer"—the

Messiah. That Jewish authorities do not translate his name in the text below, but simply transliterate it into un-interpreted Hebrew, strikes me as interesting, particularly because it invites a Christian understanding, given that the Messianic deliverer is referred to as "Wonderful Counselor," "Mighty God," "Everlasting Father" and "Prince of Peace." Jewish commentators steer readers away from the verse's natural messianic gloss with its seemingly Christological implications by seeming to intentionally obscure the language. The commentators prefer avoiding the Jesus connection by implying that the verse is a reference to King Hezekiah (p.44)—an impossibility given the nature of the person and his work described. Issues with this problematic implication aside, note that this person one day rules "upon the throne of David" with the result that "of peace there is no end"—certainly not Hezekiah. Isaiah 9:5-6 (6-7 in the Christian Bible), describes the striking inauguration of the Messianic age as follows:

> 9:5 For a child is born unto us, a son is given unto us; and the government is upon his shoulder; And his name is called "Pele-joez-el-gibbor-Abi-ad-sar-shalom";
> 6 That the government may be increased, and of peace there be no end, upon throne of David and upon his kingdom, to establish it and to uphold it, through justice and through righteousness, from henceforth even forever. The zeal of the Lord of hosts doth perform this.

Subtitled with "The Messianic Age" in our Jewish commentary (p.56), Rabbi Slotki correctly sees beyond Hezekiah and draws upon Rashi's authority to note the reference to the "Messiah ben David"—the Messiah Son of David (p.56). This comes naturally, given that in 11:1-16, Isaiah explicitly prophesies that the Messiah will be of Davidic stock (v.1) and that the power of the Holy Spirit will be strongly evident in Him (v.2). Power will be manifested too, say Judaism's sages, by virtue of His "intellectual, administrative and spiritual attributes respectively" (p.55). A predicted end to wars revolving around the "holy mountain" (v.9) is happily one of the fruits of His eventual administration. This, itself, is construed as being an allusion to the eventual cessation of tempestuous activities in and around Jerusalem (p.58), at some future point in time when, to use the prophet's poetic language, "the wolf shall dwell with the lamb, and the leopard shall lie down with the kid" (v.6). Peace will one day predominate and "the earth will be full of the knowledge of the Lord as the waters cover the sea." When? Isaiah says that the Messianic "root of Jesse" will be established first, with the result that "him shall the nations seek" in verse 10c (also, 65:19-25) in a restored earth.

> 11:1 And there shall come forth a shoot out of the stock of Jesse, and a twig shall grow out of his roots. 2 And the spirit of the Lord shall rest upon him, the spirit of wisdom and understanding, the spirit of counsel and might, the spirit of knowledge and of the fear of the Lord…
>
> 6 And the wolf shall dwell with the lamb, and the leopard shall lie down with the kid; and the calf and the lion and the fatling together; and a little child shall lead them…
>
> 8 And the suckling child shall play on the hole of the asp [cobra], and the weaned child shall put his hand on the basilisk's [viper's] den. 9 They shall not hurt nor destroy in all my holy mountain; for the earth shall be full of the knowledge of the Lord as the waters cover the sea. 10 And it shall come to pass in that day, that the root of Jesse, that standeth as an ensign for the peoples, unto him

> shall the nations seek, and his resting place shall be glorious."

Lest his readers perhaps become too contented by visions of an eventual end of hostilities and a happy national restoration and exaltation at day's end, in chapter 24 the prophet Isaiah speaks to precursory wars and concomitant miseries—of a period of national calamities and of consequential dire tribulations. Judaism's sages correctly note that this is but an introduction, and that chapters 24-27 combined "form a distinct group of oracles, strongly marked by their general apocalyptic character. They speak of God's desolating judgment of the world, the terrors of that great day, the suppression of the power of evil in heaven and on earth, the consequent blessings upon Israel and humanity, the abolition of death for ever and the wiping of tears from all faces" (p.110). God, say Judaism's interpreters, here calls for "retribution" (p.110), given that all have transgressed (v.5) both His revealed and His moral laws (p.111). "Sadness and desolation prevail" as houses and gates will be in ruins and/or simply deserted (p.111), with Jews scattered among the nations where they are despoiled (p.112). This passage depicts that the earth must "pass through tribulation and sorrow" before God's visitation, and that it must experience "catastrophic manifestations" and "convulsions" prior to experiencing God's renewed favor (p.113). The sun's eclipse is noted by commentators, an event that is construed as "destined to take place prior to the Messianic era" (p.114).

> 24:1 Behold, the Lord maketh the earth empty and maketh it waste, and turneth it upside down, and scattereth abroad the inhabitants thereof… 3 The earth shall be utterly emptied, and clean despoiled; for the Lord hath spoken His word.

> 4 The earth fainteth and fadeth away, the world faileth and fadeth away. The lofty people of the earth do fail.
>
> 6 …a curse devoured the earth… the inhabitants of the earth waste away, and men are left few.
>
> 11 There is crying in the streets… All joy is darkened, the mirth of the land is gone. 12 In the city is left desolation, and the gate is smitten unto ruin.
>
> 19 The earth is broken, broken down, the earth is crumbled in pieces, the earth trembleth and tottereth; 20 the earth reeleth to and fro like a drunken man… 21 The Lord will punish… the kings of the earth upon the earth. 22 And they shall be gathered together as prisoners are gathered in the dungeon… 23 The moon shall be confounded and the sun ashamed; for the Lord of hosts will reign in mount Zion and in Jerusalem.

Not minded to leave His people in such dire straights forever, in 26:21 the Lord's coming to redeem humankind is noted. "Behold, the Lord cometh forth out of His place, to visit upon the inhabitants upon the earth their iniquity," is an activity rightly interpreted by the rabbis to be a shift "from His attribute of mercy to that of [His] judgment" (p.122). That His expressed purpose is to both destroy the devil (depicted by Isaiah as a serpentine creature) and to redeem His people is evidenced by the poetic language which follows in 27:1—an apocalyptic image that will excite New Testament prophecy students who are familiar with the picture of Christ's eventually grabbing hold of and condemning Leviathan in Rev. 20:1-3. A few interpretations of the "Leviathan" are offered by Jewish commentators; the view of the "dragon" noted is particularly interesting because it is said by Jewish sages to possibly hark back to Tyre on the Mediterranean (p.122) where, in Isa. 23, the King of Tyre is referred to, and understood as, "Lucifer" by Jewish exegetes (p.69).

> 27:1 In that day the Lord with his sore and great and strong sword will punish Leviathan the slant serpent, and Leviathan the tortuous serpent; and He will slay the dragon that is in the sea.

God's coming to bring judgment is noted elsewhere, for example chapter 30, which expresses it in different, though equally powerful terms. That the judgment was promised "long ago" is underscored by Judaism, as is its being of a "catastrophic" nature (p.146), one described by a perpetual fire with "smoke continuously rising from it" (p.147).

> 30:27 Behold, the name of the Lord cometh from afar, with His anger burning, and in thick uplifting of smoke; His lips are full of indignation, and His tongue is as a devouring fire; 28 And His breath is as an overflowing stream…

> 30b …With furious anger, and the flame of a devouring fire, [He will come] with the bursting of clouds, and a storm of rain, and hailstones.

In much the same manner, at the closing of the book in chapter 66, Isaiah is on record noting God's coming fury which precedes the inauguration of the Messianic era: "Dire tribulation will be the lot of the apostates, while eternal peace will be the reward of the faithful," say Judaism's sages (p.319). Noted here is a major war whereby "the Lord contends" and takes "vengeance upon His enemies" (p.324) with the result that "the slain of the Lord are many." "All nations and tongues" are said to be participants in the horrific debacle and its aftermath. Israel's dispersed are noted principally, given God's re-establishment of them in their own land, as a testimony of His greatness to the surrounding nations, all of whom are gathered to see His manifest glory and strength revealed through Israel's restoration. (35:1-7; 43:1-7; 51:2-10; 52:11; 54:5-11; 60:1-4, 10-16) Reference to a "new heaven and earth" is made in conjunction with His redemption and steadfast love for Israel, as is mention of God's enemies burning in a fire that will not be quenched, construed by Judaism's sages as a reference to "Ghenna" (p.324)—what Christians typically refer to simply as "Hell."

> 66:15 Behold, the Lord will come in fire, and His chariots shall be like the whirlwind, to render His anger with fury, and His rebuke with flames of fire. 16 For by fire will the Lord contend, and by His sword with all flesh; and the slain of the Lord will be many.
>
> 18 … I will gather all nations and tongues; and they shall come, and shall see my glory. 19 And I will work a sign among them, and I will send such as escape of them unto the nations, to Tarshish, Pul and Lud, that draw the bow, to Tubal and Javan… 20 And they shall bring all your brethren out of all the nations… to my holy mountain Jerusalem…
>
> 22 For as the new heavens and new earth, which I will make, shall remain before Me, saith the Lord, so shall your seed and your name remain. 23 And it shall come to pass, that from one new moon to another, and from one Sabbath to another, shall all flesh come to worship before Me, saith the Lord. 24 And they shall go forth and look upon the carcasses of the men that have rebelled against Me; for their worm shall not die, neither shall their fire be quenched; and they shall be an abhorring unto all flesh.

Summary

Revealed through these and other Isaiah passages is an "end of days" scenario, which comes with abysmal circumstances on diminished earth. God is seen as coming from heaven to war against the "Leviathan" and to establish His kingdom. In this regard, Isaiah speaks of the much-hoped-for cessation of global hostilities, coming at "day's end," in the context of which he draws readers' attention to the coming "Root of Jesse" who will, one day, sit upon the throne of David, with the result that peace will be established finally. That the anticipated peace comes on the heels of war is an oft-repeated theme in Isaiah. Word of precursory agonies precedes the coming ecstasies. Isaiah tells of God's coming to unleash angst and fury; that all humankind will have to reckon with the disconcerted Judge. With scores settled, Isaiah says that Israel will be restored, that the nations will be judged, that sinners will be punished and he refers to a "new heaven and earth," which is followed by an unpleasant picture of God's enemies suffering torment in an unquenchable fire. All this and more is found in Isaiah—as elsewhere with the Old Testament.

Ezekiel

Rabbi Dr. S. Fisch construes Ezekiel 36 (the message of the 'dry bones') to be the "brightest in the whole book" (Ezekiel, p.238) in part because a newly-constituted Israel is predicted by Ezekiel, one that will receive "a new heart" and a "new spirit" in verse 26, what Rabbi Fisch reminds is the actual Holy Spirit of God (p.246). Chapter 37:1-14 follows with an "inspiriting" message to the exiles that prophetically tells of (1) a miraculous resurrection from exile and consequential misery, of (2) deliverance from sin through "cleansing," of (3) the appearance of a Davidic-type shepherd in verse 24—whom Rabbi Fisch, in keeping with Jewish tradition, construes as the Messiah (p.251)—of (4) an everlasting "new covenant" of peace, (5) recognized by the nations of the earth and (6) headquartered out of Jerusalem, what Fisch construes as another reference to the Messianic era (p.252).

> 37:1 The hand of the Lord was upon me, and the Lord carried me out in a spirit, and set me down in the midst of a valley, and it was full of bones… 4 Then He said unto me: "Prophesy to these bones… 5 Behold 'I will cause breath to enter ye and ye shall live.'" 11 Then He said unto me: "Son of man, these bones are the whole house of Israel…." 12 Prophesy and say unto them: Thus saith the Lord God: I will open your graves… and bring you into the land of Israel… 14 And I will put my spirit in you and ye shall live….
>
> 21 …Behold, I will take the children of Israel from among the nations, whither they are gone, and will gather them on every side, and bring them into their own land; 22 and I will make them one nation in the land… 23 [and I will] cleanse them; so they shall be My people and I will be their God. 24 And my servant David shall be king over them, and they all shall have one shepherd; they shall also walk in Mine ordinances, and observe My statutes and do them….
>
> 26 Moreover, I will make a covenant of peace with them—it shall be an everlasting covenant with them; and I will establish them, and multiply them, and will set My sanctuary in the midst of them for ever… 28 And the nations shall know that I the Lord sanctify Israel, when My sanctuary shall be in the midst of them for ever.

Israel's restoration, we're told, does *not* go unchallenged—indeed, God's will never does. Here, while reflecting upon chapters 37-38, Rabbi Fisch reminds his traditional Jewish readers that "the character of the two chapters is apocalyptic and relates to the indefinite future, the advent of the Messiah" (p.253). This notion is supported by the expression "last days" which is used more than once, as you'll see. Chapter 37 speaks cryptically of God's prompting Gog and Magog to raise their hoary heads against the covenant people, after which time God gets the better of them, with the result that His might is acknowledged globally. Fisch informs, "In Rabbinic literature, Gog and Magog are frequently referred to as the leaders of a hostile army against Israel before the coming of the Messiah" (p.253).[8]

Owing to the following passages, and others, Judaism's sages envision that there will be a great struggle at day's end—one of worldwide proportions. They see in this Ezekiel text a portent of that coming worldwide struggle, that it will be played against a reconstituted nation-state of Israel, and that God is victorious at day's end. As you'll see in 38:5 the text refers to "Persia" explicitly, in the conflagration; in conjunction with this, Rabbi Fisch notes that "Gomer"[9] (v.6), was read in Talmudic times as "south Persia" (p.254). In Sura 18, the Koran tells that Alexander the Great built a wall around Gog and Magog to exclude them from the world, and that, after being excluded for so long, Gog will once again make its entrance—for war!

Reproduced below are samplings of the English renditions of the Hebrew texts referenced above.

---

[8] He goes on to say that "[t]he Midrash Tanchuma [a Jewish scriptural commentary] interprets *Gog-u-Magog* to mean the assembly of enemy nations, pointing out the numerical value of the two Hebrew words is seventy, the supposed number of peoples in the ancient world" (p.253).

[9] This Gomer is a person different from Hosea's wife.

38:1 And the word of the Lord came unto me, saying: 2 "Son of man, set thy face toward Gog, of the land of Magog, the chief prince of Meshech and Tubal, and prophesy against him, 3 and say: Thus saith the Lord God: Behold I am against thee, O Gog, chief prince of Meshech and Tubal; 4 and I will turn thee about, and put hooks in thy jaws, and I will bring thee forth, and all thine army… 5 Persia [Parthia/Iran], Cush, and Put with them… 8 After many days thou shalt be mustered for service, in the later years thou shalt come against the land that is brought back from the sword, that is gathered out of many peoples, against the mountains of Israel, which have been a continual waste; but is brought forth out of the peoples….

15 "And thou shalt come from thy place out of the uttermost parts of the north, thou, and many peoples with thee… a great company and a mighty army; 16 and thou shalt come against My people Israel, as a cloud to cover the land; it shall be in the end of days, and I will bring thee against My land, that the nations may know me, when I shall be sanctified through thee, O Gog, before their eyes…

19 "…Surely in that day there shall be a great shaking in the land of Israel… 21 …every man's sword shall be against his brother.

39:1 "And thou, son of man, prophesy against Gog, and say: '…Behold I am against thee, O Gog… 4 Thou shalt fall upon the mountains of Israel, thou, and all thy bands… [and] I will give thee unto the ravenous birds of every sort and to the beasts of the field, to be devoured. 6 And I will send a fire on Magog.' 8 Behold, it cometh,

> and it shall be done; this is the day whereof I have spoken [during which time I will destroy Israel's enemies].
>
> "[Now] 27 … [I] am sanctified in them in the midst of many nations. 28 And they shall know that I am the Lord, in that I caused them to go into captivity among the nations; and have gathered them unto their own land; and I will leave none of them any more there; 29 neither will I hide My face any more from them; for I have poured out my spirit upon the house of Israel, saith the Lord."

Zechariah

Zechariah is keen on speaking of God's Spirit being poured out upon His people. In 39:29 (above), Ezekiel says as much, and also in 36:26 where he likewise speaks of a coming "new spirit." For these and other reasons, Judaism's sages believed that "in the Messianic age the spirit of prophecy will be restored to Israel" (Ezekiel, p.265). Zechariah says much the same.

Rabbi Eli Cashdan says that "Zechariah is rich in Messianism" (Zechariah, p.268), as it tells of the day when "the shoot" (see Isa. 11:1) will rule. "This Messiah," says Cashdan, "is incomparably greater than he could see in Zerubbabel and Joshua"—who led Israel in his day; for this Messiah, says he, "will make an [eventual] entry into Jerusalem, and in his day the 'new Jerusalem' will arise as the capital of the Kingdom of God on earth, to which the nations of the world will flow and join themselves to the God of Israel and to His people" (p.268).

Before the ecstasy, however, agonies are sadly predicted. Jews regathered to their ancestral homeland (Israel) will be subjected to the horrors of war, once more; and it will get the better of them. In the wake of heathen armies' successes round about, the capital city, Jerusalem, is made the object of attack by the godless hordes bent on Israel's demise. Zechariah sees Jerusalem surrounded by alien armies, with no hope of victory—at least not a hope that's visible right away. God, Himself, is said to then make His entrance and present as Israel's Deliverer, the long anticipated "Messiah." Interestingly, however, He is recognized as one who had been "thrust through" previously (v.10b); this, say the Talmudic rabbis harks to "the Messiah son of Joseph who will fall in battle," but who, obviously, rises again (p.321-322) as noted here.

> 12:2 Behold, I will make Jerusalem a cup of staggering unto all the peoples round about, and unto Judah also shall it fall to be in the siege against Jerusalem. 3 And it shall come to pass in that day, that I will make Jerusalem a stone of burden for all the peoples… And it shall be that all the nations of the earth shall be gathered against it…
>
> 7 The Lord shall save the tents of Judah first, that the glory of the house of David and the glory of the inhabitants of Jerusalem be not magnified above Judah. 8 In that day shall the Lord defend the inhabitants of Jerusalem… 9 And it shall come to pass in that day, that I will seek to destroy all the nations that come against Jerusalem. 10 And I will pour upon the house of David and upon the inhabitants of Jerusalem, the spirit of grace and supplication, and they shall look upon Me, because they have thrust him through…

Summary

What can we conclude from our casual assessment of Jewish reads on the aforementioned prophetic texts? For one, Jews perceived that Old Testament prophets were given to telling about a day when God would manifest Himself in power and strength. In advance of His doing so, however, the world was predicted by all to fall into abysmal straits. Things are predicted to go particularly bad for a restored Israel—at least at the first. In due time, however, the biblical prophets and their Jewish interpreters seem happy to report that the Messiah will come and deliver His people from the godless masses bent on their destruction.

Prophecies in Jewish Apocalyptic Literature

Iran in Ancient Prophecy[10]

Assisted by various ancient, post-biblical authors, we now examine how the final conflict discussed in the previous section was described as a future war played out between east and west—and a war that is not just about Israel, though it is played out in Israel. *We will discover how the west-east conflict served as the classic prophetic model for the climactic battle between European-Roman based forces and Arabian-Eastern ones, brought into the region for war.* Israel, as we shall see, will be drawn into the middle.

As noted previously, Roman and Iranian/Parthian cultures clashed on more than one occasion. In one case particularly, Rome was quite humiliated. As with the aforementioned biblical prophets, ancient religious personalities spoke about these events. Some of these post-biblical commentators were called "sibyls."

Professor J. J. Collins noted that, "The sibyl is always depicted as an aged woman uttering ecstatic prophecies."[11] Dr. Collins also said that many of these so-called prophets

---

[10] As noted previously, I've employed here *Old Testament Pseudepigrapha*, published by Doubleday (1983), and edited by the Princeton scholar Professor James Charlesworth.

[11] Culled from James Charlesworth's Old Testament Pseudepigrapha, Vol. I (Garden City, NY: Doubleday, 1983), p. 317.

were "Asiatic" sorts "who came to Greece from the East,"[12] notably from what would be known as modern Iran today. The Persian/Parthian prophetic oracles are noted first in the ancient texts,[13] where predicting "woes and disasters upon mankind," centered around wars, seems to have been a common feature of the oracles—perhaps owing to Old Testament biblical influences noted above. Often the doomsday soothsaying is "directed against specific peoples and cities."[14] In this regard, Dr. Collins further opined that "the theme of conflict between East and West [seems] a favorite subject of the Sibylline Oracles"[15]—much as these perennial tensions reverberate today, as we are all too aware.

What are we to make of these non-biblical oracles? You will have to consider what impression they make upon you. For his part, Professor Collins expressed his belief in their importance, noting that the "oracles represented a remarkable attempt to find a mode of expression common to Jews (or Christians) and gentiles."[16]

What will readers find? Predictions of (1) an Iranian-based invasion of Judea that is (2) thwarted by God's intervention; (3) predictions of the transformation of an increasingly disoriented planet with (4) the planet's final destruction by fire at day's end.

Directly related to our interests is Collins's opinion on the following—a point that will be developed in some detail, given its relevance to Iran/Parthia and Armageddon: "The

---

12 Ibid.
13 Ibid.
14 Ibid., p. 318.
15 Ibid., p. 319.
16 Ibid., p. 322.

most famous example" of future prophecy, says Dr. Collins, "is the legend that Nero would return as an eschatological adversary at the head of a Parthian [invading] host."[17] This is the Sibylline's version of the New Testament's Battle of Armageddon, where the world's most inherently evil personality leads a demonized charge against civilization! Particularly interesting is the fact that *ancient writers believed an Iranian end-time invasion to be a given.* Follow below where I offer direct text quotes and give reference addresses for those wanting to check my sources.

Book 4 of the *Sibylline Oracles* predicts that "The power of the Persians[/Iranians] will be the greatest of the whole world" (4:60). Noted shortly thereafter is an oft-repeated prediction that "an evil storm will also come upon Jerusalem" and that a "great king will flee from Italy like a runaway slave… over the channel of the Euphrates… beyond the Parthian land" (4:115-120)—the defector being construed as the Emperor Nero, himself the personification of demented evil. From there—from Iran!—"the strife of war being aroused will come to the west… having crossed the Euphrates with many myriads" (4:137-139). Book 4 further predicts that "when faith in piety perishes from among men, and justice is hidden in the world… [then] there will be a fire throughout the whole world, and a very great sign with sword and trumpet… The whole world will hear a bellowing noise and a mighty sound. He will burn the whole earth, and will destroy the whole race of men… He will destroy everything by fire" (4:153-179).

Book 5 reads much the same as Book 4. It notes that "the Persian will come into your soil like hail, and he will destroy your land" (5:93-94), and that the advance will be led by the Italian defector noted above: "[T]he one who obtained the

---

17 Ibid., p. 323.

land of the Persians will fight, and killing every man he will destroy all life… But when he attains a formidable height and unseemly daring, he will also come, wishing to destroy the city of the blessed ones, and then a certain king sent from God against him will destroy all the kings and noble men" (5:101-109) who gathered against the city of the blessed ones—Jerusalem and the Jews.

That destruction will be visited upon Iran/Persia is noted later, when scorn is cast upon them. "Go East, to the mindless tribes of the Persians, and show them what now is and what will be" (5:113-114), when a "great [and extremely wicked] king of Rome, a godlike man from Italy, will cut the ridge of the Isthmus… come to the Medes and to the kings of the Persians… lurking with these evil ones against a true people" (5:138-149). It goes on to say that "There will come to pass in the last time about the waning of the moon a war which will throw the world into confusion and be deceptive in guile. A man … will come from the ends of the earth in flight and devising penetrating schemes in his mind. He will destroy every land and conquer all… He will destroy many men and great rulers… For fire will rain on men from the floors of heaven, fire and blood, water, lightening bolt, darkness, heavenly night, and destruction in war, and amidst over the slain will destroy at once all kings and noble men" (5:361-380).

Equally poetic and forceful are the oracles noted in Book 8. The book opens with "As the great wrath comes upon the disobedient world, I [will] show forth the wrath of God to the last age, prophesying to all men, city by city" (8:1-3). A diabolical leader will come and "ravage the race of peoples, undistinguished tribes, the nation of the Hebrews… when he comes from Asia"—Parthia/Iran (8:140-141, 146). He will be thwarted, however; for "dark blood will pursue the great beast… and he will [eventually] pass over to Hades" in defeat (8:158-159).

Let's now step back for a moment and ask the following: What do we note from a casual reading of these oracles?

The quote "The power of the Persians will be the greatest of the whole world" notes an expectation that a wicked eastern empire will factor significantly at day's end. "An evil storm will also come upon Jerusalem" suggests that Israel will be caught up by the eastern empire's advances "over the channel of the Euphrates" as does "the strife of war being aroused will come to the west… having crossed the Euphrates." Book 4's prediction that "there will be a fire throughout the whole world, and a very great sign with sword and trumpet… [and] He will burn the whole earth, and will destroy the whole race of men… He will destroy everything by fire" sounds much like a prediction in 2 Peter 3:7 that God will do likewise. Bearing in mind particularly our discussion in Chapter 1, read again the Book 5 quotes from "the Persian will come into your soil like hail" through "a certain king sent from God against him will destroy" him, to the description of "a war which will throw the world into confusion and be deceptive in guile." Despite their secular source, they sound remarkably like a New Testament understanding, do they not?

Continuing with Book 8's description of the horrible, diabolical leader's coming from Asia—Parthia/Iran—and the warning that he will not prevail but pass over to Hades in defeat, both these square reasonably well with the New Testament's revelation of a last days' world. Iran's emergence as a formidable, extremely hostile force today, coupled with that nation's expressed intention to annihilate Israel and take on the world, strikes me as interesting—not to mention menacing—in part, because Iran's doing so seems to have been predicted long ago. Speaking of ancient predictions, here are some others I think you'll find absolutely fantastic.[18]

The First Ethiopic Apocalypse of Enoch

Introduction

The book of 1 Enoch originated in Judea and was used at the Essene community where the *Dead Sea Scrolls* were penned, just prior to the Christian era.[19] 1 Enoch comes down from antiquity in Aramaic, Ethiopic, Greek and Latin forms; but there is a cogent argument that these were translated from a Hebrew original. In any case, the book does come from an authentically Judaic milieu; and, owing to its popularity in ancient Jewish circles—it was used in Baruch, Ezra and the New Testament—it is worthy of our consideration. Likewise, this Jewish book was highly regarded by many of the Church Fathers, owing to the many points of contact between it and the New Testament.

Here, I am primarily concerned with introducing my readers to *Enoch's understanding of the termination of the present age and the inauguration of the next one.* Enoch's fantastic vocabulary is worth noting because through various visions and dialogues that he allegedly had been privileged to have with heavenly beings, an eschatological picture emerges that is very much akin to the New Testament's—even though the pseudonymous work in question pre-dates the Christian era by well over a century. We'll look at its relationship to the New Testament

---

[18] I was impressed when I stumbled upon the following ancient sources years ago, and initially reported on them in a 1994 volume entitled The Evolution of a Revolution: Reflections on Ancient Christianity in its Judaistic, Hellenistic and Romanistic Expressions, published by University Press.

[19] E. Isaac, 1 (Ethiopic Apocalypse of) Enoch, in The Old Testament Pseudepigrapha, Vol. I, p. 8.

later; let's begin by looking at the story firsthand. I will briefly reconstruct 1 Enoch's eschatological scenario(s), then I will examine various passages from 1 Enoch.

Reconstruction of the Eschatology of 1 Enoch

Arrangement of Material

In the latter days, earth dwellers will be thrust into a period of tribulation. This horrific period will terminate at the Messiah's advent (1 Enoch 91:5-17). The natural order will be thrown out of kilter, and there will be an apparent change of the times and seasons (80:2-8). At the beckoning of angels, the kings of the earth will be gathered together for battle—akin to our Armageddon; finally they will be destroyed (56:5-8) by the "Son of Man" (the "Messiah"), who is instrumental in both provoking and terminating the final conflict (46:1-5).

Readers are told that God will visit Mount Zion with his holy army, and rescue the "chosen" people from the clutches of the wicked (1:1-9). He will proceed to give to both the righteous and the wicked their just rewards: life and death eternal, respectively (62:1-14; 103:4-8). With the overthrow of the dark and oppressive forces, power will be transferred to the meek, who will go on to inherit the earth (5:7; 38:3-5). The righteous will rejoice, while the wicked writhe in agony.

The "Head of Days" (God) will sit on his throne and the judgment books will be opened (47:3) by him who will judge even the secrets of men's hearts (49:4). Those who spoke evil against God will be thrust into hell (27:2). Fallen angels will be sent to the abyss (18:9-19:3): Enoch is specifically informed that they will be chained and carted off to destruction (54:1-6; 56:1), that it's a place of never-ending torment (21:7-10), and that it's an eternal oven (98:3).

Eternal life will be granted to the just (71:13-17); and they, being those who have their names inscribed in the Book of Life, are promised to shine like the stars (58:2-3; 104:1-4).

There will be a new heaven and a new earth (45:3-6). Man and animal alike will rejoice in the earthly regeneration that attends the Messianic era (51:4-5); and the nations of the world will pay homage to the victorious "Son of Man" during His ministration on the rejuvenated planet (48:1-10).

Throngs will gather around the enthroned Lord and forever sing His praises (14:16-23; 39:10-13). There will be good reason to offer up continual, jubilant praise to the Lord; for planted in Paradise will be a tree with a fragrance that causes sorrow and sickness to cease (25:3-7): in short, members of the regenerated commonwealth will enjoy a cessation of all evils—finally, genuine felicity!

A Closer Look at 1 Enoch

Having outlined what I believe to be the basic flow of events in Enoch's ancient eschatology, it remains to be seen whether or not my understanding can be borne out by a cursory reading of the texts themselves. Owing to the fact that the above-mentioned themes are repeated a number of times and in various contexts, I took the liberty of *not* producing the passages in the order that they appear in 1 Enoch, preferring a topical approach instead.[20] I felt that a thematic approach—as reflected above and outlined below—would be more helpful. It remains for my readers to determine whether or not they feel my model is helpful. Expecting that you'll be

[20] For those interested, here is their order of appearance in the text: 1:1-9; 5:7; 10:13-11:2; 14:16-23; 18:9-19:3; 21:7-10; 25:3-7; 27:2; 38:3-5; 39:10-13; 45:3-6; 46:1-5; 47:3; 48:1-10; 49:4; 51:4-5; 54:1-6; 56:1-8; 58:2-3; 60:7; 24; 62:1-14; 69:26-29; 71:13-17; 80:2-8; 91:5-17; 98:3; 103:4-8; 104: 1-4.

pleased, and saving judgment for later anyway, I invite you to attend to the passages themselves, noted immediately below following their italicized headings.

An Introduction to the General Scheme

Enoch envisions that *planet earth will fall into a tumultuous period of great tribulation* and that *this period will come to an end with the advent of the Messiah* (91:5-17).

> [I] know that a condition of oppression will grow strong on the earth, and great punishment will be completed over the earth... and again injustice will be repeated... And then injustice and sin and reviling and oppression and all the deeds will increase, and falling-off and reviling and uncleanness will increase; there will be a great punishment from heaven upon them all, and the holy Lord will come forth in anger, and with punishment, that he may pass judgment on the earth. And in those days oppression will be cut off from its roots... the roots of injustice will be cut off, and the sinners will be destroyed with the sword, and the roots of the revilers will be cut off in every place... And the first heaven will pass away and cease, and a new heaven will appear, and all the powers of heaven will shine to eternity... there will be many weeks without number, to eternity, in goodness and in justice, and sin will not be mentioned from that time on to eternity.

During the last days—in other words, during the period of dire tribulation—there will be an apparent *changing of the times and seasons* (80:2-8).

> And in the days of the sinners the years will be shortened... the fruit of the earth will be tardy... the moon

> will change her order and will not appear in her time... And many leaders of the stars of command will err, and they will change their paths and deeds, and those subject to them will not appear on time....

Wars are decreed! At the beckoning of angels, the *kings of the earth will be gathered together for battle, with particular mention of Parthia/Iran*; finally they will be utterly destroyed (56:5-8) by the "Son of Man" (the Messiah), who will visit the earth for that very purpose (46:1-5).

> And in those days the angels will assemble, and turn their heads toward the east, toward the people of Parthia and Media, in order to excite the kings, and that a disturbance come over them from off their thrones, that they come forth from their resting places like lions, and like hungry wolves amidst their flocks. And they will ascend and step upon the land of their chosen, and the land of his [God's] chosen will be before them [and they will be defeated]... And in those days [after the battle] the mouth of Sheol will be opened, and they will sink into it; and their destruction, Sheol, will devour the sinners from the presence of the chosen.

And,

> And there I saw one who had a head of days [was old], and his head was white like wool; and with him was a second whose countenance was like the appearance of man... And I asked one of the angels, who went with me, and who showed me all the secrets, concerning this son of man, who he was and whence he was, and why he goes with the Head of Days? And he answered and said unto me: This is the Son of man, who has justice, and justice dwells with him, and all the treasuries of secrets he

> reveals, because the Lord of the spirits has chosen him, and his portion overcomes all things before the Lord of the spirits in rectitude to eternity. And this Son of man, whom thou hast seen, will rouse the kings and mighty from their couches, and the strong from their thrones, and will loose the bands of the strong, and will break the teeth of the sinners. And he will expel the kings from their thrones and from their kingdoms, because they do not exalt him and praise him, and do not acknowledge humbly whence the kingdom was given to them.

God will visit his Mount with his army, and *He will rescue the "chosen" people from the clutches of the wicked* (1:2-9).

> The Holy and Great One will come from his abode, the God of the world. And from there he will step on Mount Sinai, and appear with his hosts, and appear in the strength of his power from heaven... And the earth will be submerged, and everything that is on the earth will be destroyed, and there will be a judgment upon everything, and upon all the just. But to the just he will give peace, and will protect the chosen, and mercy will abide over them, and they will all be God's and will be prosperous and blessed, and the light of God will shine for them. And behold, he comes with myriads of the holy to pass judgment upon them, and will destroy the impious, and will call to account all flesh for everything the sinners and the impious have done and committed against him.

He will then give to both the righteous and the wicked their *just rewards*: life and death eternal (62:1-14; 103:4-8).

> Open your eyes, and lift up your horns, if ye are able to recognize the Chosen One. And the Lord of the spirits sat on the throne of his glory... and the word of his mouth slew all the sinners and all the impious, and they were destroyed before his face... [The wicked] will look one upon another, and will tremble and cast down their countenances, and pain will seize them, when they see this Son of woman sitting on the throne of his glory... For formerly the Son of man was hidden, and the Most High preserved him before his power, and has revealed him to his chosen. And all the powerful kings and exalted and they who rule the earth will fall before him upon their faces, and will worship and will hope in this Son of man, and will petition him and ask him for mercy [but to no avail.]... And the angels of punishment will receive them to take vengeance on them, because they abused his children, his chosen... the sword of the Lord of the spirit is drunk with them... [Of the righteous] ...the Lord of the spirits will dwell over them, and they will dwell with this Son of man, and will eat and lie down and rise again with him to all eternity.

And,

> And your souls will live, ye who have died in justice, and your spirits will rejoice and be glad, and their remembrance will be before the face of the Great One to all the generations of eternity... [And of the wicked] Do you know that their souls will be caused to descend into Sheol, and it will be ill with them, and their trouble great. And in darkness and in toils and in a burning flame their spirits will burn at the great judgment; and a great judgment will be for all generations to eternity.

And,

> [F]or the chosen there will be light and joy and peace, and they will inherit the earth, but for you the impious there will be a curse. And when the secrets of the just shall be revealed, then the sinners will be judged, and the impious will be expelled from the presence of the just and chosen. And from that time those who hold the earth will not be powerful and exalted, nor will they be able to behold the face of the just, for the light of the Lord of the spirits is seen on the face of the just and chosen. And the mighty kings will perish at that time, and will be given over into the hands of the just and holy.
>
> And there was great joy among them, and they blessed and honored and exalted, because the name of the Son of man had been revealed to them... [Sitting upon his throne] he [the Son of man] causes to disappear and to be destroyed the sinners from the face of the earth. They shall be bound with chains and shall be imprisoned in the assemblage place of destruction....
>
> And in those days they will be led to the abyss of fire, in torture and in prison they will be locked for all eternity... they will be burned together from now on to the end of all generations… all wicked deeds shall cease, and the planet of justice and righteousness shall appear... justice and righteousness will be planted in joy forever. Then all the just will bend the knee, and they will remain alive till they beget a thousand children, and they will complete all their days of their youth and their Sabbath in peace. And in those days the whole earth will be worked in justice, and will all be planted with trees, and will be full of blessings. And all the trees of desire will be planted on it,

> and vines will be planted on it; the vine planted on it will bear fruit in abundance. And all the seed sown on it in one measure will bear ten thousand, and one measure of olives will make ten presses of oil. And cleanse thou the earth of all oppression and injustice and all sin and all wickedness and all uncleanness which are produced on the earth: eradicate them from the earth. And the children of men shall become just, and all the nations shall worship me as God, and bless and all will worship me. And the earth will be cleansed of all corruption and all sin and all punishment and all torment, and I will never again send a flood upon it, from generation to generation, to eternity. And in those days I will open the storerooms of blessings which are in heaven, in order to bring them down upon the earth, upon the deeds and labor of the children of men. Peace and rectitude will become associates in all days of the world, and in all generations of the world.

Condemnation for the Wicked and the Eternal Bliss for the Righteous

The *"Head of Days" (God) will sit on his throne* and the *judgment books will be opened* (47:3) by him who will judge even the secrets of man's heart (49:4).

> I saw the Head of Days, as he sat upon the throne of his glory, and the books of the living were opened before him, and his whole host, which is in high heaven and around him, stood before him… And he will judge secrets…

Those who blaspheme will be thrust into hell (27:2).

> [Said the angel Uriel to Enoch:] "This cursed valley is for those who will be cursed for eternity, and here will be

> assembled all those who have spoken with their mouths unseemly words against God...; here they will be assembled, and here will be their judgment…"

Fallen angels will be sent to the abyss (18:9-19:3).

> And I saw a burning fire which was in all the hills. And there I saw a place, beyond the great earth... And I saw a great abyss in the earth, with columns of heavenly fire... The angel said: "This is the place of consummation of heaven and earth; it is a prison for the stars of heaven, and for the host of heaven... they who have transgressed the command of God... he was enraged at them, and bound them till the time of the consummation of their sins in the year of mystery." And Uriel said to me: "Here will stand the souls of those angels who have united themselves with women, and having assumed many different forms, have contaminated mankind, and have led them astray so that they brought offerings to demons as to gods, namely on the day when the great judgment, on which they will be judged, shall be consummated. And their women having led astray the angels of heaven, will be like their friends." And I, Enoch, alone saw this vision, the ends of all; and no man has seen them as I have seen them.

Enoch is specifically informed that *evil angels will be chained and carted off to destruction* (54:1-6; 56:1).

> And I looked and turned toward another side of the earth, and I saw there a deep valley with a burning fire. And they brought the kings and the powerful and put them into the deep valley. And there my eyes saw how they make instruments for them, iron chains of immense weight. And I asked the angel of peace, who went with me, saying:

> "These chain instruments, for whom have they been prepared?" And he said to me: "These have been prepared for the hosts of Azzazel, to imprison them and put them into the lowest hell... [Good angels] will throw them on that day into the oven of burning fire, that the Lord of the spirits may avenge himself on them on account of their injustice, because they became subject to Satan, and have led astray those who dwell on earth." And I saw there the hosts of angels of punishment walking and holding chains of iron and metal.

Hell is a place of never-ending torment (21:7-10; 98:3).

> And from there I went to another place which was still more terrible than the former. And I saw a terrible thing: a great fire was there, which burned and flickered...; it was bounded by a complete abyss, great columns of fire were allowed to fall into it... And at that time I said: "How terrible this place is, and painful to look at!" At that time answered Uriel, one of the holy angels, who was with me: "Enoch... this is the prison of the angels, and here they are held in eternity."

And,

> [I]n shame and in murder and in great poverty their spirits will be cast into an oven of fire.

Eternal life will be granted to the just (71:13-17).

> And the Head of Days came with Michael and Gabriel, Rafael and Panuel, and with thousands and with ten thousand times ten thousand angels without number. And

> the angel came to me and said: "Thou art a son of man who was born to justice, and justice dwells over thee, and the justice of the Head of Days will not depart from thee." [Peace to those, his chosen]...long life will be with the Son of man, and peace will be to the just, and his right path to the just, in the name of the Lord of the spirits to all eternity.

Those who have their names inscribed in the Book of Life (the Chosen) will shine like the stars (58:2-3; 104:1-4).

> Blessed are ye, the just and chosen, for your portion is glorious. And the just will be in the light of the sun, and the chosen in the light of everlasting life. I swear to you, just ones, that in heaven the angels will have a remembrance concerning you for good before the glory of the Great One. Your names will be written before the glory of the Great One... ye will shine like the luminaries of heaven, and will be seen, and the portals of heaven will be opened to you... Hope, and do not cease your hope, for ye will have great joy, like the angels in heaven.

New Heavens and a New Earth

There will be a *new heaven and a new earth* (45:3-6).

> On that day the Chosen One will sit upon the throne of glory... on that day I will cause my Chosen One to dwell among them, and will transform heaven and make it a blessing and a light eternally. And I will transform the earth and make it a blessing, and will cause my chosen ones to dwell thereon; and those who have committed sins and crimes will not step on it... for the sinners there awaits before me a judgment, that I may destroy them from the face of the earth.

The *earth will rejoice in the regeneration* that accompanies the Messianic era (51:4-5).

> And in those days the mountains will skip like rams, and the hills spring like lambs satisfied with milk, and they will all be angels in heaven. Their faces will shine in gladness, because the Chosen One has arisen in those days, and the earth will rejoice, and the just will live thereon, and the chosen will walk and move thereon.

Defeated nations will finally pay homage to the victorious Son of Man—the Messiah (48:1-10).

> And at that place [Paradise] I saw an inexhaustible fountain of justice... And at that hour that the Son of man was called near the Lord of the spirits, and his name before the Head of Days... All who live upon the earth will fall down before him and bend the knee to him, and will bless and praise him and sing songs to the name of the Lord of the spirits. For this purpose he was chosen and hidden before him before the world was created, and he will be before him to eternity... for in his name they will be saved... And on the day of their trouble, there will be rest on the earth; before him they will fall and not rise again, and there will be no one to take them with his hands and lift them up, because they have denied the Lord of the spirits and his Anointed.

Throngs will gather around the enthroned Lord, and forever sing His praises (14:16-23; 39:10-13).

> [I]ts floor was fire... and its ceiling was also a flaming fire. And I looked therein and saw a high throne; its appearance was like the hoar-frost, and its circuit like a shining sun and voices of the Cherubim. And from under the great throne came streams of flaming fire, and it was impossible to look at it... None of the angels were able to enter, nor any flesh to look upon the form of the face of the Majestic and Honored One. Fire of flaming fire was round him, and a great fire stood before him, and none of those who were around him could approach him; ten thousand times ten thousand were before him... And the holy ones who were near him did not leave day or night....

> Before him there is no ceasing... Thee they praise who do not sleep; they stand before thy glory, and bless and glorify and exalt thee, saying: "Holy! Holy! Holy! the Lord of the spirits fills the earth with spirits." And here my eyes saw all those who do not sleep, standing before him, and they say: "Blessed art thou, and blessed be the name of the Lord to all eternity."

There will be good reason to offer up continual, jubilant praise; for *planted in Paradise is a tree with a fragrance that causes sorrow and sickness to cease* (25:3-7). In short, members of the regenerated commonwealth will enjoy a cessation of all evils—*at last there will be genuine peace and happiness!*

> [Michael the archangel answers Enoch's inquiry about the special tree in paradise]... And this tree of beautiful fragrance cannot be touched by any flesh until the time of the great judgment; when all things will be atoned for and consummated for eternity, this will be given to the just and the humble. And its fruits will be given to the chosen;

> it will be planted towards the north, in a holy place, toward the house of the Lord, the Eternal King. Then they will rejoice greatly, and be glad in the Holy One; they will let its fragrance enter their members, and live a long life upon the earth, as thy fathers lived; and in their days no sorrow or sickness or trouble or affliction will touch them. Then I blessed the Lord of glory, the Eternal King, because he had prepared such for the just men, and had created such....

Summary of 1 Enoch

I see an eschatological picture emerging that is very much akin to the New Testament's: note the dire "Tribulation" Period during which time wickedness/lawlessness increases. There is a changing of the times and seasons. As is the case with the New Testament, in Enoch we learn of the advent of a Messiah who will come and make war with the wicked in a climactic battle, and with Parthian/Iranian forces, resulting in the termination of the period of Tribulation and the arrival of a long-anticipated "Messianic Era," replete with the longed-for age of peace and tranquility. Following this, Enoch says there will be a judgment, at which time God, called the "Ancient of Days," will give to everyone their recompense: the wicked will be cast into the netherworld to spend eternity engulfed in a lake of fire; the "chosen" and "just" will enjoy eternal bliss on a new heaven and a new earth.

Having observed all of this—and more—in 1 Enoch, we will now consider how other Jewish commentators likewise employed this imagery. Specifically, we will go on to consider 4 Ezra.

Fourth Book of Ezra
Introduction

Although it is commonly known in the English as 2 Esdras, the text in view will be referred to as 4 Ezra from its Latin name *Esdrae liber IV*. The Latin and Oriental versions seem to rely on an underlying Greek text; however, there is good reason to believe that the Greek text was a translation of a Semitic original—Aramaic or Hebrew[21]—as with the Enoch text above. 4 Ezra really comes in two parts: chapters 1-2 and 15-16 (the beginning and end) are likely interpolations added by a Christian redactor;[22] chapters 3-14 consist of assorted dialogues and visions regarding the fate of Israel, sin, suffering, death, judgment of the wicked, the "heavenly Zion," the Messiah, and the "end of the age." The scholarly consensus is that this Jewish text was composed around 100AD, thus making it contemporaneous with parts of the New Testament and no relation to the prophet Ezra of the Old Testament. Dr. Bruce Metzger, professor of New Testament language and literature at Princeton University, opines that similarities between 4 Ezra and the New Testament abound.[23] As was the case with my treatment of 1 Enoch, here again I will first provide my readers with my reconstruction of the book's essential eschatology, after which I will then attend to the texts firsthand.

---

21 See Bruce Metzger, "The Fourth Book of Ezra," *The Old Testament Pseudepigrapha,* Vol. I., pp. 519-520.

22 See Dr. W. Sanday's preface in G. H. Box's The Ezra Apocalypse (London: Sir Isaac Pitman & Sons, 1912), p. 5; and Bruce Metzger, "The Fourth Book of Ezra" The Old Testament Pseudepigrapha, Vol. I., p. 517.

23 Dr. Metzger lists the following examples: 4 Ezra 7:7 and Matt. 7:13 (i.e., the narrow gate to paradise); 4 Ezra 8:3 and Matt. 22:14f; Lk. 13:23f (i.e., the saying, many were created but few will be saved); 4 Ezra 4:33 and Matt. 24:3; Lk. 21:7 (i.e., the question, how long will it be till the end?); 4 Ezra 7: [61] and Jms. 4:14.

Reconstruction of the Eschatology in 4 Ezra

Arrangement of Material

4 Ezra takes up soteriological questions[24] related to humanity's vitiation[25], and redeemed mankind's eventual entrance into an eternal reward. Sin is understood to have entered the stage of the human drama through the "First Adam" (4 Ezra 3:21-22). Like the first man, all have sinned (8:35), and as a result of this perfidy, few will inherit the world to come (8:1-3). It is not God's will that any would perish (8:59), and so salvation is made available to all. Interestingly, as in the New Testament, entrance into the eternal bliss is awarded to those who walk the "narrow way" (7:6-16).

In addition, 4 Ezra reflects an eschatological scenario very much akin to that of 4Q 286, the famous "Son of God Scroll" in the Dead Sea Scroll collection. Mindful of a termination of the present era, 4 Ezra tells of the particulars of the "end of the age" (6:7). Jews are informed that a period of unprecedented tribulation is predicted (4:51-5:3). Salvation is promised to those who endure the tribulation (6:25). The Messiah will come after the tribulation, in accordance with the signs; and His Kingdom will be manifest (7:26-28). There are a host of end-time expressions employed, like: "number being fulfilled," "times and seasons," and "appointed" times and more.

Similarities abound with the New Testament. For example, 4 Ezra 12:42 is similar to 2 Pet. 1:19 (given the view that prophecy is akin to a lamp shining in a dark place) and 4 Ezra 13:1 is akin to 2 Thess. 2:8 (where the Messiah's destruction of the wicked is pictured). The above mentioned tribulation-deliverance scenario

---

[24] Questions concerning the biblical doctrine of salvation; the definition of soteriology is "spiritual salvation, especially by divine agency"

[25] Defilement.

is reiterated and expanded upon in 4 Ezra: Ezra goes on to tell of specific signs in advance of the Messianic era (9:1-6); he speaks about the appearance of a terrible kingdom in the last days (12:13); and he informs that the Messiah will eventually destroy the nefarious hordes, thus displacing the evil kingdom and inaugurating a period of eternal bliss. Preliminary considerations aside, let's now attend to the particulars and see how this is the case.

A Closer Look at 4 Ezra

Humanity's Corruption and Personal Salvation

Sin is said to have entered the stage of the human drama through the *"First Adam"* (3:21-22).

> ...the first Adam, clothing himself with the evil heart, transgressed and was overcome; and likewise all who were born of him. Thus the infirmity became inveterate....

All mankind is defiled; *all have sinned* (8:35).

> For in truth, there is none of the earth-born who has not dealt wickedly, and those that exist who has not sinned.

As a result of this perfidy, *few will inherit the world to come* (8:1-3).

> This age the Most High has made for many, but the age to come for few... Many have been created, but few shall be saved!

It is not God's will that any would perish (8:59).

> For the Most High willed not that men should come to destruction.

Salvation is available. Entrance into the eternal bliss is awarded to those who walk the *narrow way* (7:6-16).

> There is a builded city which lies on level ground, and it is full of good things; but its entrance is narrow and lies on a steep, having fire on the right hand and deep water on the left; and there is only one path lying between them both, that is between the fire and the water (and so small) is this path, that it can only contain one man's footstep at once. If, now, this city be given to a man for an inheritance, unless the heir pass[es] through the danger set before him, how shall he receive his inheritance? And I said: It is so Lord! Then said he unto me: Even so, also, is Israel's portion; for it was for their sakes that I made the world; but when Adam transgressed my statues, then that which had been made was judged: and then the "ways" of this world became narrow and sorrowful and painful and full of perils coupled with great toils. But the ways of the future world are broad and safe, and yield the fruit of immortality. If, then, the living shall not have surely entered into these narrow and vain things, they will not be able to receive what has been reserved for them.

Eschatology: The Tribulation and Messianic Eras

There are a host of *end-time expressions* employed in this Jewish apocalyptic literature: for example, "number being fulfilled," "times and seasons," and "appointed" times (4:36-37).

> And to them the archangel Jeremiel made reply, and said: Even when the number of those like yourself is fulfilled!

> For he has weighed the age in the balance, And with measure has measured the times, and by number has numbered the seasons….

Mindful of a termination of the present era, people ask for the particulars of the *"end of the age"* (6:7).

> Then I answered and said: What shall mark the parting asunder of the times? When shall the End of the first (age) and beginning of the second be?

Jews are informed that a period of unprecedented *tribulation* is predicted (4:51-5:3).

> Then I made supplication and said: Thinkest thou that I shall live until those days? Who shall be in those days? He answered me, and said: As for the signs concerning which thou askest me... Behold the days come when the inhabitants of the earth shall be seized with great panic, and the way of truth will be hidden, and the land of faith be barren. And iniquity will be increased above that which thou seest or that thou hast heard of long ago. And the land that thou seest shall be a pathless waste; and men shall see it forsaken....

Salvation is promised to those who *endure* the tribulation (6:25).

> And it shall be that whosoever shall have survived all these things that I have foretold unto thee, he shall be saved and shall see my salvation and the end of my world.

The *Messiah will come after the tribulation,* in accordance with the signs; His Kingdom will be manifest (7:26-28).

> For behold the days come, and shall be that when the signs which I have foretold unto thee shall come to pass, then shall the city that now is invisible appear, and the land which is now concealed seen. And whoever is delivered from the predicted evils, the same shall see my wonders. For my *Son the Messiah* shall be revealed, together with those who are with him....

There will then be *a resurrection* (7:32).

> And the earth shall restore those that sleep in her, and the dust those that rest therein. And the chambers shall restore the souls that were committed unto them.

There will then be *a judgment* (7:33).

> And the Most High shall be revealed upon the throne of judgment: (and then cometh the end) and compassion shall pass away (and pity be far off) and long-suffering withdrawn, But judgment alone shall remain, truth shall stand, and faithfulness triumph. And recompense shall follow, and the reward be manifest; deeds of righteousness shall awake, and deeds of iniquity shall not sleep. And then shall the pit of torment appear and over against it the place of refreshment. The furnace of Gehenna shall be manifest and over against it the Paradise of delight. And then shall the Most High say to the nations that have been raised (from the dead): Look now and consider who you have denied, whom you have not served, whose commandments ye have despised. Look now before (you) here delight and refreshment, there fire and torments!

> Thus shall he speak unto them in the Day of Judgment. For thus shall the Day of Judgment be. (A *day)* whereon there is neither sun, nor moon, nor stars, neither clouds, nor thunder, nor lightning, neither wind, nor rain-storm, nor cloud-rack, neither darkness, nor evening, nor morning;…

> Measure the matter carefully in thy mind, and when thou seest that a certain part of the predicted signs are past, then shalt thou understand that it is the very time when the Most High is about to visit the works which he has made. When in the world there shall appear quaking of places, tumult of peoples, scheming of nations, confusion of leaders, disquietude of princes, then shalt thou understand that it is of these things the Most High has spoke since the days that were aforetime from the beginning. For just as with respect to all that has happened in the world the beginning is obscure, but the end (issue) manifest, so also are the times of the Most High: the beginnings are [visible] in portents and secret signs, and then end in effects and marvels.

A *terrible kingdom makes its appearance in the last days* (12:13); but the victorious Messiah displaces the evil kingdom.

> Behold the days come when there shall arise a kingdom upon the earth, and it shall be more terrible than all the kingdoms that were before it.

> And after this I beheld, and Lo! all who were gathered together against him to wage war with him were seized with great fear; yet they dared to fight. And lo! when he saw the assault of the multitude as they came he neither lifted his hand nor held spear nor any war-like weapon;

> but I saw only how he sent out of his mouth as it were a fiery stream, and out of his lips a flaming breath, and out of his tongue he shot forth a storm of sparks. And these were all mingled together—the fiery stream, the flaming breath, the storm of sparks...and they fell upon the assault of the multitude which was prepared to fight, and burned them all up, so that suddenly nothing more was to be seen of the innumerable multitude save only the dust of the ashes and the smell of smoke. When I saw this I was amazed.

Messiah/God's Son delivers the godly.

> Behold the days come when the Most High is about to deliver them that are upon the earth. And there shall come astonishment of mind upon the dwellers on earth: and they shall plan to war one against the other, city against city, place against place, people against people, and kingdom against kingdom. And it shall be when these things shall come to pass, and the signs shall happen which I shewed thee before, then shall my Son be revealed whom thou didst see as a man ascending... But he shall stand upon the summit of Mount Sion. [And Sion shall come and shall be manifest to all men, prepared and builded, even as thou didst see the mountain cut out without hands.] But he, my Son, shall reprove the nations that are come for their ungodliness... and then shall he destroy them without labor by the law which is compared to a fire.

Summary

A cursory examination of the material in 4 Ezra discloses that there are indeed relationships between Jewish soteriology and eschatology and similar doctrines reflected in the New Testament. Lastly, in what follows, we'll consider the Apocalypse of Baruch's testimony, wherein we will also note the relationship between ancient "Jewish" and "Christian" understandings.

The Apocalypse of Baruch

Introduction

Dr. A. F. J. Klijn, writing an introduction about this Apocalypse in *Old Testament Pseudepigrapha,* alleges that there are three reasons why the work in question originated in Israel: (1) there was a Hebrew original of the work; (2) close relationships existed between Baruch and rabbinic literature; and (3) the author of the work—certainly not Baruch himself, who was a disciple of Jeremiah in 590BC—took his stand with Jews residing in Judea and encouraged Jews in the Diaspora. Though the destruction of Jerusalem was given as the occasion for the writing, it is generally understood that the text was written after 70AD, making it a contemporary of some of the New Testament books.

The writer was interested in the Temple; this, according to Klijn, served as a suitable starting point for his questioning Israel's fate given that it was now without a sacred Sanctuary. Israel's destiny is of paramount importance to the author. In what follows, I will focus on Baruch's eschatological vision in general, and his vision of Messianic redemption in particular.[26]

---

[26] Klijn went on to outline the book as follows: 1:1-8:8, Destruction of Jerusalem by the Babylonians; 9:1-12:4, Baruch's Lamentation Following his Fast; 12:5-20:4, Questions about Righteousness and Avoiding Corruption; 20:5-30:5, Baruch's Predictions: Disasters are Coming, the Messiah's Coming follows, as does the Resurrection of the Dead and a Final Judgment; 31:1-34:1, Warning of Disaster in the End of Days; 35:1-43:3, Vision of the Forest; 44:1-46:7, Baruch Speaks on God's Judgment; 47:1-48:50, Baruch's

Reconstructing Baruch's Eschatology

Arrangement of Material

To summarize Baruch, the earth's inhabitants will be seized with terror, pressed from all sides during the Tribulation (Bar. 25:1-4), a period that comes replete with: commotions, death, desolation, famine, earthquakes, terrors, portents, oppression and wickedness (27:1-15). During this period there will be a multiplication of wars, rumors of wars and assorted cataclysmic events (48:31-39). Hatred will greatly increase, wars and murders will be commonplace, treachery will become normative, and people will devour one another (70:2-10). Wickedness will escalate through a succession of evil kingdoms, the last of which will be more nefarious than the previous ones: it will be the kingdom of the wicked ruler of the period of Great Tribulation—an anti-Messiah. Finally, the Messiah will come, destroy the wicked and bring the period to a close (39:3-7).

The Messiah's arrival will bring an end to the earthly hostilities. Upon His advent, the world will experience rejuvenation (29:3-8). A resurrection of the dead will also accompany His coming. This assemblage of the deceased will occur at what Baruch calls "the consummation of the times" (30:1-3). There will be a judgment with adjudication based on how folk treated the "Seed of Jacob" (72:2-4). The perfidious leader of the tribulation kingdom will also be judged (40:1-3). Some will be saved—by their "works," according to the apocalypse—and they will be delivered from the Tribulation, shine like the stars, inherit Paradise and more (51:7-14). With

---

Understanding of God's Predetermination; 49:1-52:7, The Outward Appearance of the Righteous after the Resurrection; 53:1-74:4, The Vision of the Cloud with Bright and Dark Waters; 75:1-77:26, The Saving of the Righteous; 78:1-87:1, An Exhortation to Faithfulness to the Jewish Tribes in the Dispersion (Ibid., p. 615).

the judgment of the world complete, the Messiah will bring about a period of peace and prosperity—the long anticipated "Messianic era." Sin, death and disease will vanish; man and animal will exist peacefully, side by side. In short, the creation will return to the state that existed in the Garden of Eden—Paradise restored (73:1-7).

A Closer Look at Apocalypse of Baruch

Dire Tribulation

The earth's *inhabitants will be panic-stricken*, pressed from all sides *by a dire Tribulation Period that ends with the Messiah's arrival* (25:1-4).

> Thou too shalt be kept safely till that time till that sign which the Most High will work for the inhabitants of the earth in the end of days. This therefore will be the sign. When a stupor shall seize the inhabitants of the earth, and they shall fall into many tribulations, and again when they fall into great torments. And it shall come to pass when they say in their thoughts by reason of their much tribulation: "The Mighty One doth no longer remember the earth"—yea, it will come to pass when they abandon hope, that the time will then awake.

The Tribulation Period comes replete with: commotions, death, desolation, famine, earthquakes, terrors, portents, oppression and wickedness (27:1-15). And *there will come a succession of evil kingdoms, the last of which will be more nefarious than the first.* Finally, however, *the Messiah will come, destroy the wicked and close the period* (39:3-7).

And He answered and said unto me: "Into twelve parts is that time [the Tribulation Period] divided... In the first part there will be the beginnings of commotions. And in the second part (there will be) slayings of great ones. And in the third part (there will be) the fall of many by death. And in the fourth part the sending of desolation. And in the fifth part famine and withholding of rain. And in the sixth part earthquakes and terrors... multitude of portents and incursions... fall of fire... rapine and much oppression... wickedness and unchastity... Confusion and the mingling together of those things aforesaid... [this period is called, then] the consummation of the times."

Behold! The days come, and this kingdom will be destroyed which once destroyed Zion, and it will be subjected to that which comes after it. Moreover, that also again after a time will be destroyed, and another, a third, will arise, and that also will have dominion for its time, and will be destroyed. And after these things a fourth kingdom will arise, whose power will be harsh and evil far beyond those which were before it... And by it the truth will be hidden, and those who are polluted with iniquity will flee to it... And it will come to pass when the time of his consummation when he should fall has approached, then the principate of My Messiah will be revealed, which is like the fountain and the vine, and when it is revealed it will root out the multitude of his host.

... it will come and pass by with quick vehemence, and it will be turbulent coming in the heat of indignation. And it will come to pass in those days that all the inhabitants of the earth will be moved one against another... For there will not be found many wise at that time, and the

> intelligent will be but a few... And there will be rumors and tidings not a few, and the works of portents will be shown... many will be roused in anger to injure many, and they will rouse up armies in order to shed blood, and in the end they will perish together with them. And it will come to pass at the self-same time, that a change of times will manifestly appear to every man... Therefore a fire will consume their thoughts... for the Judge will come and will not tarry.
>
> But those who have been saved by their works... they will behold the world which is now invisible to them, and they will behold the time which is now invisible to them... they shall be made like the angels, and be made equal to the stars, and they shall be changed into every form they desire, from beauty into loveliness, and from light into the splendor of glory. For there will be spread before them the extents of Paradise, and there will be shown to them the beauty of the majesty of the living creatures which are beneath the throne, and all the armies of the angels, who are held fast by a command, that they may stand in their places till their advent comes. Moreover there will then be excellency in the righteous surpassing that in the angels. For the first will receive the last, those whom they were expecting, and the last those of whom they used to hear that they had passed away. For they have been delivered from this world of tribulation, and laid down the burden of anguish.

During the Tribulation Period hatred will greatly increase, wars and murders will be commonplace, as treachery becomes normative: people will devour one another (70:2-10).

> Behold! The days come, and it will be when the time of the age has ripened, and the harvest of its evil and good seeds has come, that the Mighty One will bring upon the earth and its inhabitants and its rulers perturbation of spirit and stupor of heart. And they will hate one another, and provoke one another to fight, and the mean will rule over the honorable… it will come when those things which were predicted have come to pass, that confusion will fall upon all men, and some of them will fall in battle, and some of them will perish in anguish, and some of them will be destroyed by their own. Then the Most High will reveal to those peoples whom He has prepared, and they will come and make war with the leaders that shall then be left. And it shall come to pass that whosoever gets safe out of the war will die in the earthquake, and whosoever gets safe out of the earthquake will be burned by the fire, and whosoever gets safe out of the fire will be destroyed by famine. [And it will come to pass that whosoever of the victors and the vanquished gets safe out of and escapes all these things aforesaid will be delivered into the hands of My servant Messiah.] For all the earth will devour its inhabitants.

Finally, *the Messiah will come and judge the nations of the earth* on the basis of how they treated God's Old Testament covenant people—the "Chosen People," the Jews (72:2-4).

> After the signs have come, of which thou wast told before, when the nations become turbulent, and the time of My Messiah is come, He will both summon all the nations, and some of them He will spare, and some of them He will slay... Every nation which knows not Israel,

and has not trodden down the seed of Jacob, shall indeed be spared.

And it will come to pass when all is accomplished that... the Messiah will then begin to be revealed. And Behemoth will be revealed from his place, and Leviathan will ascend from the sea, those two great sea monsters which I created in the fifth day of creation, and I kept them until that time... The earth will also yield its fruit ten thousand fold, and on one vine there will be a thousand branches, and each branch will produce a thousand clusters, and each cluster will produce a thousand grapes, and each grape will produce a core of wine. And those who have hungered will rejoice: moreover, also, they will behold marvels every day... the treasury of manna will again descend from on high, and they will eat of it in those years, because these are they who have come to the consummation of time.

And it will come to pass after these things, when the time of the advent of the Messiah is fulfilled, and He will return in glory, then all who have fallen asleep in hope of Him shall rise again. And it will come to pass at that time that the treasuries will be opened in which is preserved the number of the souls of the righteous, and they will come forth, and a multitude of souls will be seen together in one assemblage of one thought, and the first will rejoice and the last will be grieved. For he knows that the time has come of which it is said, that it is the consummation of the times....

The perfidious Tribulation Period leader is judged (40:1-3).

> The leader of that time will be left alive, when the multitude of his hosts will be put to the sword and be bound, and they will take him up to Mount Zion, and My Messiah will convict him of all his impieties, and will gather and set before him all the works of his hosts. And afterwards he will put him to death... And his [God's] principate will stand forever, until the world of corruption is at end, and until the times aforesaid are fulfilled.

> And it will come to pass, when He has brought low everything that is in the world, and has sat down in peace for the age on the throne of His kingdom, that joy will then be revealed and rest appear. And then healing will descend in dew, and disease will withdraw, and anxiety and anguish and lamentation will pass from amongst men, and gladness will proceed through the whole earth. And no one shall again die untimely, nor shall any adversity suddenly befall... And wild beasts will come from the forest and minister unto men, and asps and dragons will come forth from their holes to submit themselves to a little child. And women will no longer have pain when they bear, nor will they suffer torment when they yield the fruit of the womb.

Summary

Given that there are striking similarities between these and New Testament predictions, one is forced to offer an accounting for the relationships. Speaking to this issue, Professor Donald Hagner, of the Fuller Theological Seminary, said that "The rabbis and Jesus share[d] the expectation of a coming eschatological kingdom of God to be realized on earth. The nature of the kingdom would have been agreed on essentially, if not altogether, by the rabbis and Jesus."[27] The agreement motif seems especially significant to me. The selected samplings in this chapter show that Dr. Hagner is correct. We shouldn't really be surprised that similarities exist; for both ancient Christians and ancient Jews alike shared the same Old Testament. In that it contains eschatological reflections of a period of tribulation, a coming Messiah, a messianic era, and a final judgment, one could reasonably expect that Jewish Bible teachers would pick up on these themes, as they had.

As we know, the idealized age of global peace and spiritual regeneration, so beautifully articulated in the Old Testament era(s) was never realized during the Old Testament period(s). The Jewish Bible closes with a host of unappeased longings and unfulfilled prophecies. The prophets envisioned a time, in the future, when the Glory of the Lord would shine forth upon (and from) a regenerated people, resting securely in their Promised Land—in Israel (Hosea 3:4-5; Jer. 23:5-6; Ezek. 37:24-28; Zech. 8:7-8). Israel's "faithful" waited (and await still, for that matter) for the renewal of the once-splendid, though short-lived, Davidic Empire—to later be ruled by the Messiah Himself. The prophets knew that in advance of the promised Messianic era the earth's inhabitants would undergo a series of global upheavals, major wars, etc. (Zech. 12:1-14:21; Dan. 11:1-45), but that peace would eventually come when the Prince of Peace arrived. He, the Messiah, would bring about a cessation of global hostilities (Isa. 2:4, for one); additionally, He would inaugurate a period of global regeneration (Amos 9:13-14; Ezek. 34:26-29) and even a resurrection of the dead would accompany it (Dan. 12:2). In

---

27 Donald Hagner, *The Jewish Reclamation of Jesus* (Grand Rapids: Academie Books, 1984), p. 140.

sum, under His administration it was envisioned that the earth would experience a period of total health and healing (Isa. 33:24; 35:5-6) resulting, of course, in great joy and peace (Isa. 51:11). For these and many other reasons, *I see Jesus' message as fitting well within the boundaries of first-century Jewish apocalyptic language.*

Jesus spoke to a Jewish audience and employed linguistic images that were discernable to His Jewish hearers. Prior to His departure, He told of His return and, in the process, noted that He'd enter a world wracked with miseries, wars and a host of attendant despairs.

Iran's place in that downward spiraling, last days' world is made apparent in a few biblical texts worth noting. Persia's explicit mention as a participant in Ezekiel's famous Gog and Magog battle against Israel (Chapters 38-39, esp. 38:5) lends credence to the proposition that Iran is an active player in the last days, as is Daniel's frequent mention of Persia being at odds with Greeks in chapters 8-12. In addition to these explicit references, Iran's participation in the Battle of Armageddon, as told in Rev. 16:12-16, factors foremost in my thinking and, with the above, paints a picture of a world that bears similarities to our present one.

IV

The *Face of* Jesus in the Iranian-Armageddon Conflict and in Ancient Jewish Eschatology

Introduction

Having heard from a variety of sources, I would like to focus this final chapter on the book of Revelation. Bringing the "Revelation" into a conversation on Bible prophecy is appropriate; in fact, it would be inexcusable to write a book on prophecy without considering John's voice in the Revelation. Given Revelation's teaching that the Armageddon conflict opens with forces staged east of the Euphrates making a final and fateful assault in and on Israel (16:12-15), and given Iran's presence just east of the Euphrates and her ubiquitous threats to assault Israel (and the West by association), it seems not just appropriate, but important to consider Revelation.

In what follows, I will (1) offer an overview of the four hundred and three verses found in Revelation, by means of a brief analysis of each of the revelation's passages; then (2) I will proceed to locate and isolate the sixty-three verses where Jesus speaks directly and consider what He had to say in more detail—brief and introductory though my comments will still be. (3) I will then close with a more detailed analysis of Jesus' words by fleshing out some of His instructions germane to the following question: How ought we to be at day's end?[1]

Jesus' practical exhortations in the seemingly conjectural[2] Revelation are particularly revealing, and strike me as significant for a variety of reasons. I don't want to say what those reasons are at the outset, however, as I prefer my readers to simply follow through the chapter, discover my reasoning and, hopefully, discover Revelation afresh. With that in mind, I invite you to consider the Revelation and attend to Jesus' words as noted.

Overview of the Book of Revelation

The book of Revelation presents us with twenty-two chapters, a total of four hundred and three verses combined. Of these, sixty-three verses contain explicit Jesus statements and instructions. For example, at the book's outset one encounters Jesus saying "I am the Alpha and Omega" twice

---

[1] The Apostle Peter was concerned with this question, as well. In 2 Peter 3:3 he noted that "scoffers will come in the last days," and that they will make fun saying: "Where is the promise of His coming? For… all things continue as they were from the beginning of creation" (4). Though scoffers debunk the notion of prophecy, Peter went on to say that nevertheless "the Day of the Lord will come as a thief in the night" (10) after which he rhetorically mused, (11): "Since all these things are thus to be dissolved, what manner of persons ought we to be in holy conduct and godliness?" Interested primarily in John's answer to that question, as noted in his Revelation, I am nonetheless impressed with Peter's by way of introduction, as he stressed the importance of Christians "be[ing] found by Him in peace," and being "…[un]spot[ted] and blameless" (14). Peter isn't especially important to me here; Jesus is. I'm sure that Peter wouldn't take offense at his words being eclipsed by Jesus' statements in John's Revelation.

[2] I don't personally believe the Revelation to be conjectural, and use the term here realizing that it's the way the book is often perceived.

(1:8, 11). He followed with "I am the first and the last" (1:17b), and then expressed that He wanted John to write down the revelation of the things that "are, and the things which will take place after this" (1:19). So much for the book's beginning. Jesus ends the Revelation in chapter twenty-two with: "behold I am coming quickly!," noted three times in verses 7, 12 and 20. There is another "Alpha and Omega" reference placed between in verse 13 (also 21:6). In between the introduction and conclusion, and in conjunction with the mention of the coming Armageddon conflict in chapter sixteen (12-16), Jesus reminds us that He is "coming as a thief" and that believers ought to be ready (15). He picks up this theme at the close, stressing the importance of "keeping the words of the prophecy" (22:7), reminding that everyone will be judged "according to his work" (12), and that "I have sent My angel to testify to you these things in the churches. I am the Root and the Offspring of David, the Bright and the Morning Star" (16).

Particularly noteworthy for our purposes is that though these very Spartan samplings of Jesus' statements are indeed exciting and worthy of much reflection, there are actually precious few revelatory words said to come directly from His lips in Revelation, except for the moral exhortations given to angels to be delivered to the seven churches, in chapters two and three. These, in fact, account for the lion's share of His teachings. To be exact, chapters two and three account for fifty-one of Jesus' sixty-three statements—the better part of His explicit and direct contributions to the book of Revelation. Instructing through angelic intermediaries, Jesus is on record there giving seven very brief messages to seven distinct churches: beginning with the one at Ephesus (2:1-7) and then Smyrna (2:8-11), Pergamos (2:12-17), Thyatira (2:18-29), Sardis (3:1-6), Philadelphia (3:7-13) and finishing with the church at Laodicea (3:14-22).

The three hundred and forty remaining Revelation verses contain fantastic heavenly throne room images (4:1-5:14), apocalyptic decrees noting ravages being unleashed upon the earth (6:1-17), faithful Israelite witnesses of every tribe (7:1-8) and a resulting "Great Tribulation" unleashed upon the righteous, given their resolve to remain loyal to the testimony of Jesus (7:9-17). Through seven angels (8:1-6) comes notice of impending cataclysmic upheavals which follow in 8:7-9:21, as does an inserted exhortation that deliverance is on its way (10:1-7) and that John—and all believers by association—must endure and serve faithfully until such time as the deliverance arrives (10:8-11). The slaughter of two witnesses follows (11:1-10) with an appendage informing us of their consequential resurrection in verses 11-14, after which the seventh angel proceeds to proclaim the Kingdom's eventual inauguration in 11:15-19. Though the Kingdom's coming is hastening, it hasn't arrived yet.

Apocalyptic images of a woman with child fleeing from a dragon hell bent on her demise capture readers' attention in 12:1-17, as do those of horrific beasts coming from the sea (13:1-10) and earth (13:11-18), given to unleashing their pent-up fury upon those who will not accept their domain, and receive the "mark of the beast" noted in 13:17. That a select few do, in fact, bear up under the imposed pressure is noted in 14:1-13. Notice of more "woes" upon bewitched fellows follows (14-20) as does a telling of God's eventual triumph (15:1-8). The Revelation then proceeds by offering a countdown to climactic Armageddon.

Reminiscent of the "Ten Plagues" and the consequential Exodus under Moses' administration, loathsome sores are predicted to one day plague humankind in 16:2. Stories of water turning to blood follow (4-7). Men are scorched (8-9), and are disoriented by darkness (10-11). The drying up of the

Euphrates River follows, an activity that is not on par with the Red Sea crossing: in marked contrast to the Red Sea escape route, this Euphrates crossing opens the way for invading hordes staging in, and/or passing through, modern Iran to come to Israel for war. This culminates in the long-anticipated "Battle of Armageddon," (12-16), and the subsequent shaking of the seduced and defiled earth (17-21).

Noting that the vile world will be embroiled in a tempestuous conflagration, in 17:1-6 the Revelation turns to announcing the evil empire's final death blow, with the empire referred to as "the whore"—"Babylon the Great: The Mother of Harlots and of the Abominations of the Earth" (5). Unveiling the mystery behind the events follows (7-18), after which the narrative returns to unpacking Babylon's sins, and the defiled earth's by association (beginning with 18:1).

The long-anticipated "Marriage Supper of the Lamb" follows upon the heels of Babylon's demise, (19:1-10), but only after the Armageddon conflict plays itself out. At that time, "Heaven opens" (11), and the emergent Savior comes upon "a white horse" and is called Faithful and True, and in righteousness He judges and makes war. The royal personality on the white horse goes by the name "King of Kings and Lord of Lords" (16). With His gaze set on re-conquest, He sets His sights on defeating the armies assembled at Armageddon (17-21). The victorious Savior gets the better of the beast soon thereafter, and utterly destroys its army (19-21). Defeated, "the dragon, the serpent of old, who is the Devil and Satan is bound for a thousand years and cast into the bottomless pit" (20:1-3). Notice of the Kingdom's establishment follows (4-6) which, in turn, is followed by a note of a brief, unsuccessful rebellion that will be crushed (7-10). All things completed, a "new heaven and a new earth" follows in 21:1-8, along with "the great city, the holy

Jerusalem, descending out of heaven from God, having the glory of God" in verses 9-27 (esp. 10-11a). The Revelation ends with a picture of paradise restored in 22:1-5 (which harks back to paradise lost in Gen. 1-3); this in turn, is followed by exhortations to keep in the ready (6-21).

Introductory Assessment of the Book of Revelation

In the Revelation's four hundred and three verses, one encounters themes of a sin-soaked and defiled earth, of consequential global upheavals and miseries, of a wicked ruler's getting the better of the planet's vitiated inhabitants and of his abusing those who resist his sway. In like manner, themes of persecuted righteous saints patiently bearing up under the abuse are noted, as is the telling of God's making His arrival on the stage of the human drama, besting the dark forces and triumphantly establishing His Kingdom! This is the revelation! But is this revelation unique to Jesus?

As noted previously in this volume, readers should remember that these and other notions are amply attested elsewhere both in the Old Testament and in Jewish apocalyptic literature, which serves as its commentary. It is a mistake to assume that because most Christian readers first encounter these notions in Revelation that the language is unique to Revelation. Closer scrutiny bears out that the Revelation actually employs notions and vocabulary from elsewhere.

If the end-time scenario's images and language is not unique to the Revelation—and I say that it is *not*—than one may ask: What *is* particularly unique to Revelation? Or, put another way, one may ask: "Precisely what does it reveal?" The New Testament's book of Revelation is unique in revealing the personhood of Jesus and His moral exhortations!

Let me offer a very brief introduction to Jesus' revelation.

His rebuke to the church at Ephesus pointed out that their good works in His name were meaningless because they had lost their original love for each other and for Him. His exhortation to that church to return to its "first love" in 2:5 is applicable today. That the church at Smyrna was enduring persecution (9) reveals that Christ doesn't always prescribe an easy road for His people. The church at Pergamos buckling under pressure prompted the Lord to call them to "repent," (16), which reveals that believers must keep on guard, lest we fall through our indolence. His displeasure that the whore "Jezebel" was tolerated at Thyatira, (20), resulting in some of the Lord's people "commit[ing] sexual immorality" with her, is particularly revealing and parallels today's licentious world where pornography is a fifty-seven-billion-dollar-per-year industry, earning more income than all the major league sports teams combined. Jesus is revealing and warning that we must keep ourselves undefiled. That the church at Sardis carries the "name of being alive but it is dead" (3:1b), with only a few authentic believers still resident (4a), reveals that many will carry the name Christian who have long since lost the vision of what it means to be what the name implies: "Christian." He exhorts us to "be watchful and strengthen the things which remain" (2), and to "remember" Christ's instructions and to "repent" (3). The church at Philadelphia was infiltrated by outsiders (9), and His instruction underscores the importance of believers being individually faithful to the Lord, given that not all is as it might seem in the churches. The "lukewarm" Laodicean church's being "neither cold nor hot" (15-16), with the result that the Messiah will "vomit" it out, reveals the need for sincere believers to keep on guard against tendencies toward sloth and indifference.

These moral exhortations are unique revelations of Jesus and demonstrate His intimate knowledge of their hearts.

Revelation's remaining verses contain the prophetic vision we saw in the preceding Overview section: fantastic heavenly throne room images, apocalyptic decrees and predictions of ravages being unleashed upon earth; the Savior's entrance, the defeat of Satan, the Judgment of all, and Paradise restored. As previously noted, the fantastic book closes with an exhortation for the saints to keep vigilant.

Interpretation of Jesus' Instructions as Briefly Noted in the Book of Revelation

Much could be said—and has been said—about the book of Revelation. Adjudging that various eschatological themes have been sufficiently developed elsewhere in this volume (as elsewhere by others) I will give pride of place to the factors that I consider to be particularly unique to the Revelation: (1) Jesus' vision—His personal appearance in the eschaton, at "day's end"; (2) Jesus' voice—His moral exhortation to believers to not let human nature get the better of us "as we live out our days."

Jesus' Appearances in the Revelation

Securing a vision of God amidst the turbulence of trying times is an oft-repeated theme in the Revelation. John gets a supernatural vision of the apocalyptic "Son of Man" in 1:9-20. He is transported to the heavenly throne room in 4:1-11, where creatures and elders glorify God singing: "You are worthy, O Lord, to receive glory and honor and power..." (4:11). He then hears about the "Lion of the Tribe of Judah" and the "Lamb of God" in 5:5, after which he sees a lamb being adored by those assembled (9-14): "You are worthy...

for you were slain… Out of every tribe and tongue and people and nation, you have made us kings and priests to our God; and we shall reign on the earth… Worthy is the lamb who was slain to receive power and riches and wisdom, and strength and honor and glory and blessing" (9-12), culminating with: "Blessing and honor and glory and power be unto Him who sits on the throne, and to the Lamb, forever and ever" (13b).This jubilation, in turn, is followed in 7:9-17 with an even greater multitude singing: "Amen! Blessing and glory and wisdom, thanksgiving and honor and power and might be to our God forever and ever" (12), followed later by a description of the Lamb's loyal followers in a comparable interlude (14:1-5).

Lest readers be prematurely intoxicated by the heavenly bliss, the writer describes the earth's descent into an horrific abyss. The planet reels beneath imposed miseries in chapters 8 through 18, with brief mention of Armageddon in 16:12-16. Jesus emerges triumphant in chapter 19 where He comes on a white horse as "King of Kings and Lord of Lords" (19:16) with an army in tow with which He vanquishes the demonic hordes assembled for the great battle. Later, while describing the New Jerusalem in chapter 21, John notes the absence of a Temple there, given that "God Almighty and the Lamb are its temple" (22). He goes on to note that the Lamb is its light (23), and that its citizens are "those whose names are written in the Lamb's Book of Life" (27).

What might we glean from these visions of the Messiah? Though we must each answer that for ourselves, let me share what I find important.

Securing a vision of God amidst the turbulence of trying times argues for the importance of dutifully participating in inspirational worship services. Good as watching Christian television and reading books might be, nothing replaces the value of gathering together as the people of God and worshipping Him in concert—these being acts that are themselves preludes to the "exultation of the multitudes" after history plays itself out; for, as John was transported to the heavenly throne room in 4:1-11, where he heard choirs singing praise to the "Lion of the Tribe of Judah" and the "Lamb of God," so too must we be transported to places of worship and encouragement, lest we wither beneath the hot sun for failure to stay watered.

The picture of Jesus' rapturous coming on a white horse as "King of Kings and Lord of Lords" to vanquish demonic hordes inspires us to believe not only in the ultimate triumph in human history, but also in God's faithfulness toward us, helping us through vexing dilemmas that confront us today. Similarly, the description of the New Jerusalem in chapter 21, where "God Almighty and the Lamb are its temple" and its light reminds us of Christ's sufficiency. The "names written in the Lamb's Book of Life," passage shows the clear-cut essence of salvation: your name is in the Book or it's not; you're in or you're out; there is no waiting list for those still deciding whether to accept Christ's invitation, no territory between Heaven and Hell for those who want to visit on weekends only. This cannot be overstated.

Jesus' Exhortations in the Revelation

In conjunction with some uniquely revealed images Revelation contains some specific revealed instructions—particularly those noted in chapters two and three.

Jesus' exhortation to the Ephesian church to return to its "first love" (2:5) beckons us to keep our drifting natures "in check" and reveals the importance of our keeping ourselves at the ready, given the tendency for human commitment to dissipate with the passage of time.

That Christ doesn't always save us from our trials but sometimes actually leads us to them seems demonstrated by the church at Smyrna that was gracefully enduring persecution (9). Though at times hard to comprehend, it is worth noting that God leads us both to and through hard times, and beckons us to stay with Him throughout the journey and grow through the process. Revealed in Revelation is the importance of being resolute, given human nature's tendency to jettison our faith and virtue when tested by challenging circumstances and problems not easily or quickly solved.

His calling the church at Pergamos to "repent" (16) reminds us that the decision to turn from sin and to follow Christ must be played out more than once. In truth, the "sinner's prayer"[3] is a first step, with many sure to follow. Those honest with themselves realize that the struggle against sin is not a battle won in a day; but is a struggle engaged in over a lifetime. May we repent when needed, as needed. This exhortation also reveals the importance of our keeping ourselves humble, with our "garments white," and keeping ourselves sincere in our struggle against sin's advances and staining power.

That "Jezebel" was tolerated at Thyatira (20) with the result that some of the Lord's people were discovered to be "commit[ing] sexual immorality" with her, is particularly appropriate in today's over-sexed world. Let me again remind that the pornographic industry is a fifty-seven-billion-dollar-

---

[3] The sinner's prayer can take many forms, but in it the sinner tells God he recognizes his sin and his need for a relationship with God through Jesus Christ.

per-year industry in America, earning more than all the major league sports combined, not to mention the combined revenues of ABC, NBC and CBS. Add to this the horrendous examples of marital unfaithfulness in our culture—even amongst believers!—and one is forced to realize that we must take this warning seriously. Revelation stresses the importance of our keeping ourselves sexually pure, lest we grieve Christ—and others—by virtue of our refusal to successfully attend to this business.

Some perhaps well-intended Christians make it a habit to refer to some churches as being "dead" while noting that others are "alive." Being judgmental is problematic in and of itself, as noted also in Matt. 7:1-5; it is particularly problematic when the superficial criterion employed to determine life and death is little more than one's preference for a particular music or baptism style—and nothing more. That the church at Sardis carried the "name of being alive but it is dead" and that Jesus exhorted it to "be watchful and strengthen the things which remain" and to "remember" His instructions and to "repent," strongly suggests that music or Christening preference is not a criterion whatsoever by which a community's health and vitality are assessed by Christ, and thus shouldn't be factors for us. Shame on us for being so shallow! This exhortation reveals the importance of our keeping ourselves alive, by keeping vigilant and mindful of the devil's schemes, remembering Christ's instructions by staying in His Word and repenting when needed, lest we develop a hardened and judgmental heart given our refusal.

The Philadelphian church's infiltration by outsiders underscores the reality that imperfection surrounds us. Some self-righteous and stuffy Christians seem given to complaining about the imperfections of those around them. "Ah," they say, "I can't go to church for there are too many hypocrites there!" Could it be that this exhortation reveals the importance of keeping *ourselves* unspotted by the flesh, and a little less focused on the problems—be they real or imagined—of those around us? So it would seem. This is the revelation for the grumpy among us!

Many ministers have drawn attention to the "lukewarm" Laodicean church's similarity to American churches today, a reminder that those who are "neither cold nor hot" will incur the Lord's displeasure. With this realization in view, we should be prompted to be more dedicated and sincere in our practices, and willing to combat innate tendencies toward moral and religious indifference. This exhortation reveals the importance of "fighting the good fight of the faith," to use Paul's words (2 Tim. 4:7). Here—in all the messages to the seven churches in Revelation—are moral exhortations and not simply apocalyptic speculations.

The importance of this cannot be overstressed, particularly for those who think that Christ's primary purpose in inspiring the Revelation was making sure we have the correct prophecy chart in hand. I say that it is not! Christ's beginning by saying "I am the Alpha and Omega" (1:8, 11) and "I am the first and the last" (1:7b) suggests to me that Jesus has authority over time and circumstance, and can, will, and does predict both. When John wrote down the revelation of the things that "are, and the things which will take place after this" (1:19), he did so employing the language of Jewish apocalyptic—words not unique to Jesus. Unique to Revelation, however, are visions of Christ and His words of moral requirements for the Christian life, over and against mere eschatological speculations related to earthly history's unfolding accordingly to a Divinely-imposed calendar.

Jesus ending with "behold I am coming quickly!," (7, 12 and 20) and that He is "coming as a thief" (15) should press individuals to be ready, personally. His picking up this theme at the close, (1) by stressing the importance of "keeping the words of the prophecy" in 22:7, (2) by commending that the individual will be judged "according to his work" in verse 12, (3) by reminding "I have sent My angel to testify to you these things in the churches" and (4) by informing "I am the Root and the Offspring of David, the Bright and the Morning Star" (16) have interesting implications, as well.

"Keeping the words" beckons individuals to read Scripture, take note and earnestly practice what is taught therein. Reminding us that believers will be judged according to their works underscores the importance of *doing* Christianity and not just believing it intellectually. Connecting Jesus to the "Root and Offspring of David" harks back to Isaiah 11:1 where the eighth century BC prophet predicted that the Messiah would be akin to a root springing forth from Davidic stock and that, as a result of His administration, equilibrium would be restored to this disoriented planet. It also reminds the "last days" church that Jesus Christ is an Israelite, descended from Davidic stock.

In Isaiah 11:6-8, the prophet spoke of a day when "the wolf shall dwell with the lamb, and the lion shall lie down with the kid" employing poetic imagery, denoting a time when there would be an end to hostilities upon the earth. In verse 9 he picked up this very theme saying that "they shall not hurt nor destroy in all My holy mountain; for the earth shall be full of the knowledge of the lord as the waters cover the sea." With wars having ceased and with peace finally established, he noted—and here, I believe, is the Revelation connection—that "the root of Jesse, that stands for an ensign of the peoples, unto Him shall all the nations seek; and His resting place shall be glorious" (10).

When will wars cease? In simple language, *wars will cease and paradise will be restored when Israel's enthroned Jewish Messiah becomes the object of adoration of the peoples of the earth.* When folk seek Him, they will find Him, and will find the peace He offers in the process. This is God's recipe!

When Jesus' birth was first announced, angels exclaimed that there would be "Glory to God in the highest, and on earth [eventually] peace and goodwill toward men," and Simeon announced that Jesus would one day be "a light to bring revelation to the Gentiles and the glory of your people Israel" (Luke 2:14, 32). That day, of course, has yet to fully arrive, as Israel and the Gentiles have yet to universally come to terms with Israel's "Messiah."

Speaking both prophetically and poetically, and while noting the multicultural nature of the "New Jerusalem"—constituted by Jews and non-Jews—John noted in Revelation 21:24 that "[all] the nations of those who are saved shall walk in its light"—emphasis: "*nations.*" Verse 5:9 underscores the multicultural nature of the assembled saints by describing them as "redeemed... out of every tribe and tongue and people and nation," much as in 7:9-10 worshippers gather from "all nations, tribes, peoples and tongues standing before the throne and before the Lamb... crying... 'Salvation belongs to our God who sits on the throne and to the Lamb.'"

I mention this here, in conjunction with Jesus' revelations in the book of Revelation, believing that multiculturalism is (1) revealed to be very important to Israel's Messiah and that there is (2) merit to fleshing out some particularly worthy applications, as I bring all this to a close.

In Light of Revelation, How Ought We to Be in the World?

A book on Bible prophecy focusing on "Armageddon," suggesting that modern Iran seems to be the doorway through which the crisis unfolds and maintaining that—contrary to Islamic claims—Jerusalem, and Israel more broadly, is promised to the Jews, may well prompt readers to disdain Arab peoples. Against this backdrop, I ask the following: How ought we to be in the world? How ought we to envision Arabs and interact with Muslims in our world?

If you will permit me a closing comment on my prophecy book, let me say in no uncertain terms that I am convinced that *hating* is simply not an appropriate form of expression for anyone who names the Name of the Lord; and let me prophesy to you that if you are inclined to hate, your righteous indignation will do *you* more harm than it will Arabs and Muslims.

Pleased as I am to report to you on prophecy and a variety of ancillary concerns, and intending to do so as long as the Lord is kind enough to permit, know that I construe my primary ministry to be one of "reconciliation" more than "information," and certainly not one of "marginalization."

I am by God's grace now "born again," and—in some ways—part of a vast commonwealth that knows no race or class. I am not kindly disposed toward those who discriminate against Muslim people—or any other people, for that matter. I say, would that more people were "saved" and thus "grafted" into the "Olive tree," for there is room in those branches for many, many more. With a Bible in my hand and with Jewish blood in the veins of the hand that grips it and in the mind that interprets it, I unequivocally believe Israel belongs to the Jewish people, and that the Israeli state has a right to defend itself in the course of securing that possession. I was born into a "western" and "European" cultural environment and have enjoyed great benefits as result of being so fortunate. I do not take kindly to the threat to those cultural moorings from moderate or radical and authoritarian versions of Islam that appear to be over-running and threatening backslidden Europe and, if unchecked, may well do likewise in the States. I believe that the church is for everyone, that Israel has a mandate as a Jewish state and that the United States of America should resist erosion and hold onto its Judeo-Christian values, which happen to run counter to Islam's.

With Isaiah, with John the "revelator," and with the righteous who look for a better world than the one they inhabited, I look for Heaven's help in managing vexing earthly problems. That said, I say "Come Lord Jesus!" I anxiously await the day when I can walk down any and every street securely, count all men my brothers, lock hearts and hands with the redeemed of the Lord and say "Come, let us go to the house of the Lord, to the house of the God of Jacob" and, as Revelation 22:17 says, drink freely with all others who "thirst" to know God's mysterious will and ways.

Conclusion

At the book's outset, I remarked how militant Iran incessantly spews out hot anti-American and anti-Israeli rhetoric and wondered whether their doing so, combined with the imposing threat of that radical Islamic state's emerging nuclear capabilities, might give rise to the question of whether Iran has a role to play in the climactic showdown at "Armageddon." Curious, I combed through a variety of ancient biblical texts and commentary in search of an answer.

Others have presented cases of their own and I encourage you to go on the Internet and conduct your own search with the words "Iran" and "Armageddon." Don't be in too much of a hurry, however, as you'll discover a million-and-a-half entries.

In this particular volume, we began with an assessment of the "Battle of Armageddon" as noted in the New Testament's famous Revelation text. As explicitly noted in the passage, the infamous battle is to be inaugurated by forces marshaled just east of the Euphrates River—what is home to modern day Iran. Coincidence? Perhaps. Perhaps not. I personally think the connection is more than coincidence.

After briefly considering Iran in relation to the Revelation story, I then offered a variety of other related secular and religious texts.

We considered the ancient historian, Josephus, who informed that "western" Roman legions were once squarely defeated by a nation-state nestled just "east" of the Euphrates—the Parthians. We noted that these hordes fared from the land constituted by the present day Islamic Republic of Iran. In addition to their successfully taking on, and getting the better of, the dreaded Roman military apparatus, we noted how these easterners intruded into ancient Israeli politics, unseating a Roman-placed Israeli governor (Herod), an act which prompted the Roman Senate to subsequently endorse and install him as Herod, the official "King" of the Jews.

As the Christian first century dawned, western Romans and Israeli Jews alike had "an axe to grind" with these "easterners," these "barbarians" who dwelt at the ragged edge of Roman civilization. Perceived by both Jews and Romans as an uncouth lot, these "easterners" were envisioned by post-biblical prophets as being destined to lead an eventual assault against western civilization, with Israel caught in the middle. These histories and related issues were considered In Chapter 2, after which in Chapter 3 we examined a variety of other prophecy-related documents.

Prominent in our analysis were prophetic Old Testament passages in Isaiah, Zechariah, Ezekiel and others, all telling of a revived Israel at day's end and of a last days' world intoxicated with fomenting, anti-Israeli discontent.

Biblical prophets, we're told, saw Israel's emergence as a nation-state at day's end, much as they saw armies taking to the field in response to pent-up and rabid anti-Jewish angst, with the result that myriad forces bent on revived Israel's annihilation were predicted to be drawn into a final showdown. That these armies were said to be led by forces marshaled from just across the Euphrates struck my curiosity, as did explicit references to the final conflict being a showdown led by "a Parthian host"—a group coming from land occupied by modern day Iran.

Discovering an ancient legend that Emperor Nero[1] would arise and return as an eschatological adversary in a last days' war, leading a Parthian/Iranian army against Israel and the "West," fascinated me and prompted me to wonder whether there might be some connection between this and the New Testament's vision of an anti-Christ.

With this question in mind, I then expanded my inquiry. I visited a variety of ancient Jewish texts and pulled references that seem remarkably similar to New Testament ones. The ancient sources prove that, at day's end, Jews envisioned a world sinking into dire decay and despair. War is decreed! Godless and frenzied forces are marshaled and unleashed against a reconstituted Israel. Before all is lost, God Himself comes and saves the beleaguered Jews, who acknowledge Him in the process.

Does this story sound familiar? I think it sounds like Christian Prophecy 101, a college course that teaches the basics of biblical prophecy.

We then took a whirlwind tour of the book of Revelation and noted Jesus' explicit instructions to the seven churches. Far

---

[1] We discussed this legend in Chapter 3 in the 'Prophecies in Jewish Apocalyptic Literature' section, where it was found in Book 4 of the *Sibylline Oracles*.

from endorsing armchair, end-time conjecturing, Jesus seemed to encourage His followers with a host of practical instructions—His unique revelation in the Book of Revelation.

All said, what have we accomplished? Specifically, what does one walk away with after considering the above?

I believe that those interested in unfolding prophetic events in the Middle East would do well to keep a watchful eye on Iran, much as they would to keep one on Israel.

Iran's place in Israel-related prophecy is secured for a number of reasons. For one, in Ezekiel 38:5, Persia (the ancient land of Iran) is explicitly referenced as being confederate with a league of nations that invades Israel, what Ezekiel sees as a last days' war spearheaded by Gog and Magog (38-39). In chapter 8:1-14, 20-21, the prophet Daniel envisioned a ram and a goat warring with one another, construed in his text as Persia and Greece respectively—East and West. In verses 15-25, Daniel interprets the battle, one that he places at the "time of the end" in verse 17. That western Greek culture and eastern Persian culture are predicted to be at odds is interesting, to put it mildly, and should cause folk to wake up and take note.

What becomes of the clash of these titanic cultures? In this contest, Daniel says that Persia will be vanquished and that western Greek culture will gain the upper hand, with one horribly wicked ruler rising eventually. In verse 23 this "latter time" prophecy precipitates the anti-Christ's emergence (compare 8:23-26 to the beginning of 2 Thess. 2), an event that Daniel says relates to "many days in the future" (26).

That day could very well be drawing near.

Conclusion

Irrespective, prophets identify Persia/Iran as having lead roles in the unfolding of end time events leading up to history's finale. Disconcerted as we are by the unfolding of current events, on the basis of Daniel's testimony one could reasonably conclude that the Persian menace will be overcome by a westerner's triumph; but that the triumphant leader—the anti-Christ—will, in turn, eventually present more formidable problems in accordance with his own intentions. For this reason, many have predicted that the anti-Christ will be a European, not an Arab or a Muslim. I personally am undecided as of this writing. I am convinced, though, of Iran's importance for all the reasons given above.

So, how should this information affect our behavior?

Do we say: "Ah! Look at those Arabs and those Iranians forever fomenting discontent in the region. God predicted years ago that they would invest their energies against Israel, and now their intentions are being manifest—just as He said!" Personally, this is the way I am inclined to think.

What should our response be?

How ought we envision Arabs and Muslims in our world in general, and how ought we construe modern Iranians in particular? Let us close by considering these very important questions.

In answer to both questions, let me say emphatically that I am personally more given to pity than I am to hate.

Hate!? Can I do that? I think not—not anyone.

Biblical faith does not allow us to hate anyone—period. Biblical virtue does prompt pity and beckons us to have compassion on the less fortunate and deceived. For this reason, I am inclined to see masses of Palestinians, Arabs and Iranians as unfortunate souls, as individuals caught up in an unfolding drama that they really don't understand and that they simply can't control. It is bigger than they are! My heart goes out to them, and I personally bear them no ill will. I commend this posture to those with biblical faith and prefer it to Arab-bashing which has no place in any legitimate Christian constitution.

I personally have met a number of Arabs who strike me as good and decent people and who, in some cases, have impressed me as possessing more moral fiber than some professing Christians. Just like us, Arab women and men want to love and be loved, to pursue dreams and visions, to be successful and live to the fullest, to raise families, to provide for their offspring as best they can, and to leave their world a little better than they found it. Must I disdain these people out of a misguided sense of Christian commitment? No. I find the thought that I should to be utterly repulsive, personally, and simply want no part of it. I believe that Jesus forbids it, in fact.

Though these human beings are people just like us, the philosophy that drives their culture and informs the way they see the world beyond their culture is not the same as ours. While I do not disdain Arab people personally, I frankly do take issue with the religious philosophy that shapes their attitudes and behaviors and those of their culture, and I see it as inferior to the philosophy that undergirds Judeo-Christian culture.

I do not believe that all culture is the same. Ours, founded on Judeo-Christian principles and rooted in biblical revelation, is far superior to all others. Our culture breeds better fruit. Judeo-Christian culture produces democracy and stimulates innovations in art, architecture, medicine, science, literature and more. Ours enhances humanity and produces a host of Nobel Prize winners.

What have all the Arab's totalitarian regimes produced lately? They know no democracy and seem incapable of developing one. Where are all their Nobel winners? Not very discernable! What is discernable? Streams of rage, blame, and hate ooze out of their dysfunctional culture in abundance. Guided by inferior principles, Muslims can't get the better of their problems, and simply blame Jews for them.

Politically incorrect as it is, I simply do not believe that all cultures and religions are equal. Judeo-Christian culture is demonstrably built atop better principles because it produces better fruit. The biblical faith that prompts me to freely think better and live better likewise prompts me to stand for its testimonies that are better than those of other religious works.

That God gave Israel to the Jewish people as a "Promised Land" is well attested throughout Sacred Writ. Yet, because Christians are told that Jesus has gone "to prepare a place for us" *on the other side of the grave*—and not on this side of the grave—and because Christians are told that "our commonwealth is in heaven and from it we await a Savior," some of them don't understand that Jews have a biblical warrant to reside in their ancestral homeland *now*.

Why?

Again, Christians simply don't have a biblically sanctioned "Promised Land" this side of the grave—period. Given real estate "here and now" as Jews are, Holy Writ commends that Judeans bear arms in defense of that God-given real estate.

This is reasonable—and required, in fact. God is referred to as "the Lord of the armies" in the Hebrew Scriptures and the Bible is full of religious warrior heroes like Moses, David and others, all attesting to God's intention to enable His people to secure their inheritance.

Just because many sincere and well-intended Christians have trouble coming to terms with this concept, their not being able to fathom that God would give real estate to individuals and commission them to guard their inheritance doesn't make it any less true!

I believe that Bible believers should support Jews' bid to secure a foothold in Israel, much as I believe that Bible believers have reason to construe that events in the region today have prophetic and apocalyptic bearing.

If you will permit me to reiterate my closing comment from Chapter 4, let me here remind you, in no uncertain terms, that I am convinced that hating is simply *not* an appropriate form of expression for anyone who names the Name of the Lord; and let me suggest to you that if you are inclined to hate, you will do more harm to yourself than to Arabs and Muslims.

I am pleased to report to you on prophecy and plan to do so as long as the Lord permits. I envision my primary ministry to be one of "reconciliation" more than "information," and certainly not one of "marginalization."

By God's grace "born again," I am not kindly disposed toward those who discriminate against Muslim people—or against any other people, for that matter. I wish that more people were "saved" and thus "grafted" into the "Olive tree," for there is room in those branches for many, many more.

Conclusion

With the complete Bible in one hand, and with Jewish blood in the veins of the hand that grips it and in the mind that interprets it, I, in no uncertain terms, believe that Israel belongs to the Jewish people, and that the Israeli state has a right to defend itself in the course of securing that possession. This position is not born out of hate; it is born out of necessity.

Speaking of "securing" and while thinking of "necessity," as one born into a "western" and "European" cultural environment and as one pleased to have enjoyed great benefits as a result of being so fortunate, I do not take kindly to those Judeo-Christian cultural moorings being threatened by a rising moderate, or radical and authoritarian version of Islamic presence that seems to be over-running and threatening backslidden Europe and, if unchecked, may well do likewise in the States.

I believe that the fellowship of Israel's Messiah is for all, that Israel has a mandate as a Jewish state and that the United States of America should resist erosion and hold to its Judeo-Christian values, as well—which happen to run counter to Islam's. Ours is a better world, given that it's built with a better world view—a biblical one.

With Isaiah, with John the "revelator," and with the righteous who look for a better world than the one they inhabited, I look for Heaven's help in the management of vexing earthly problems.

I see heaven's help coming, even as I see Iran raising its sword and threatening Israel and the world.

All said, I say "Come Lord Jesus!"

The Iranian Menace

I anxiously await the day when I can walk down any and every street securely, count all men my brothers (Jews, Arab, African, Asian and European), lock hearts and hands with the redeemed of the Lord and say "Come, let us go to the house of the Lord, to the house of the God of Jacob."

Intoxicated by the dawning of that "day," I am less concerned about the Iranian menace because I am pleased to report that the Earth's redemption draws near.